Astrology Uncovered:

A COMPLETE GUIDE TO HOROSCOPE AND ZODIAC STAR SIGNS

Julia Steyson

© 2018

COPYRIGHT

Astrology Uncovered: A Complete Guide to Horoscope and Zodiac Star Signs

By Julia Steyson

TABLE OF CONTENTS

INTRODUCTION TO ASTROLOGY

Twenty degrees up and down from the ecliptic and celestial equator, 12-star groups can be found and the name "Zodiac" was given to them in the dawn of times. This name allegedly comes from the Greek term "zodion", which means the "animal belt", and almost all of the names in it refer to animals. A common belief is that the names of the star constellations and their groupings came from the first hunters and nomads because they needed a proven method for orientation. When the age of agriculture arrived, determining the seasons of the year became necessary, and the motion of the Sun and Moon through heavenly constellations became determining factors for the meteorological and even political successes or failures.

Archeology has found firm evidence that the early humans from prehistoric times had an understanding of celestial movements and events. Many discoveries show that people of those ages carefully watched the sky and that they had precise calendars. Those calendars mainly portrayed the motion of the Moon, the Sun, and oddly, Venus and the star system of

Pleiades. Why prehistoric men would have such an interest in aligning with the Pleiades or even Venus, no one knows, but this also raises another question. Why would prehistoric people even want to follow and measure the motion of celestial bodies to the extent that they were building huge systems of stones, and later on temples, to be able to track the Sun or other significant heavenly objects? Was it just for orientation, which is useful for hunting? Certainly not.

Astrology, together with astronomy because they were considered as one science, originated in Babylonia and Sumer. Both are considered one of the oldest natural science in the world. How come that the cradle of civilization had such knowledgeable astronomers/astrologers? If we forget about the official history for a moment and start speculating, could aliens, known as Annunakis, have taught them this art?

Scriptures mention that "angels" taught humankind the art of metallurgy, medical treatments and remedies. They even advised women how to start applying makeup and of course, they showed us how to "read the sky".

The whole area of Mesopotamia, including Babylonia, Sumer, and Assyria, is rich in archeological artifacts related to astronomical/astrological themes and many of them are dated older than 2000 BC. Babylonian priests were known for their superior knowledge about planets, stars, eclipses, and all geometrical aspects those bodies can form, which was used mainly for political predictions. Bear in mind that in those ages, there were no daily horoscopes published for the common people. Natal horoscopes were drawn just for the members of the royal families and astrology was also very useful for selecting the proper dates for building new cities or attacking enemies. This remained the norm almost until the last century because the natal charts of the "common people" were seen as absolutely unimportant.

Enuma Anu Enlil is the most famous archaeological artifact from these times. It is the compilation of 70 cuneiform tablets, which describe 7000 astronomical/astrological omens. During the following thousands of years, the science of mathematics was also developed, which was used for very precise calculations of the celestial positions and the creation of the first ephemerides. From

Babylonian times, humankind inherited the habit of naming the planets after the gods and to associate them with mythical stories.

To this day, many modern astrologers claim that the original and most precise astrology called "Eden Astrology" can still be found in the areas of Iraq and Iran, but it is extremely hard to find astrologers who are practicing this art and who are willing to teach it, because astrology is outlawed in those two countries. Myth or truth, it's still hard to discover the answer.

Astrology was brought to Egypt around the 5th century BC by the Persians. However, Egypt was an extremely developed country in those times and it's hard to believe that they didn't know about planets and stars until the Persians came to conquer them. Whatever the case may be, Alexander the Great founded Alexandria and by the second century BC, this town became the location of the most famous university in the world. Ptolemy wrote an extensive work, *Tetrabiblos*, about the planetary characteristics, exaltations, triplicities, and many other basic facts. In those moments astrology, as we know it today, was born. Horoscope charts were made and analyzed in a very similar way as they are done today.

The knowledge about the stars was widely spread across the Greek territories and it was recognized as Chaldean (Babylonian) art. It continued to spread, naturally, over the whole Roman Empire and when the great kingdom fell, knowledge about astrology remained a secret

While the dark ages held power over Europe, the world of Islam continued the tradition of Alexandria's Great school. Many scholars went east, running away from rising the Christian dogma against natural sciences. The city of Baghdad became the new center of knowledge and many sciences in the forms as we know them today were founded there. The Arab world researched methodically so-called "fixed" stars and their influence on the life of our planet, and classified the system of calculating mutual relations between celestial bodies, which is known today as "Arabic parts".

When we look at the east, we are amazed by the levels of knowledge Indian or Hindu astrology achieved.

The first notion of this art can be found in Vedas, which claimed to be the oldest known texts. By the times of Alexandria's greatest breakthroughs, Vedic astrologers had to deal with higher mathematics and very serious and precise astronomical observations. The legend goes that the ancient sage Bhrigu, one of the Saptarishis (seven sages who helped to create the universe), has all the horoscope charts of all people who were born and will be born on this planet.

Due to its close relation with astronomy Vedic or Hindu astrology deals with sidereal positions of planets and uses somewhat different types of aspects, while the meaning of all celestial bodies, zodiac signs and houses are the same as they are in the "western" school of astrology.

Chinese tradition is known for its concepts of yin and yang, and it uses somewhat different types of calculations, but astrology is present there from the ancient times and besides the popular Feng Shui, which deals with the energies of the Earth, Ba Zi art deals with heavens.

Over the Atlantic Ocean, Olmec and the Aztecs were known for their calendars and precise mathematical calculations when it comes to the position of our planets, especially Venus and, as you can guess, a constellation of Pleiades. However, later on, the Mayan calendar became the most recognized and famous calendar in the world.

Back in Europe, it didn't take a long time for astrology together with astronomy to rise again. Until seventeenth century, science was necessary if you wanted to become a doctor, for instance. All diagnostics and healing treatments were done according to the planets and stars. A Christian church wasn't so satisfied with this fact, but it was powerless due to the popularity and the cautious approach of astrologers in those ages.

However, when the era of humanism and education came, astrology was pronounced the occult science, or better yet, something which is not science at all. From that moment in time, it was separated from astronomy. An interesting fact is that Isaac Newton, the father of modern scientific thought, was the one to passionately love and study astrology.

A few hundred years have passed and astrology is back again. With the rise of modern psychology, astrology took a somewhat different turn, interpreting the planetary aspects through the inner or emotional states of human beings. Luckily, after decades of vague readings, astrology returned to its roots again, and as such, interprets the outer events and envisions the future.

Mistakes happen, indeed, but if the astrologer during the reading can see around 75-80% accurately your past, present and future events, challenges, losses, and triumphs, then you have found a quality consultant and you can count on that person to be your greatest ally for the planning of your future. Let's just not forget the words of JP Morgan: "Millionaires don't need astrologers, but billionaires do".

With this in mind and if you are interested in learning something more about yourself, you will find this book extremely useful, because it will help you to see clearly what are the meanings of the planets, signs, and houses in the horoscope chart and how to recognize your character, future challenges and even how to use those challenges for your success. This can be applied to all people and the most important part is that you will be able to predict the outcome of your relationships with others. You will also learn something about myths related to ancient gods and perhaps even have a little fun.

PLANETS

Through the eyes of astrology, our lives are determined by celestial bodies; such as, fixed stars, meteor showers, various flying objects and so on, but to be able to read astrological charts, you have to learn the basic traits of the main heavenly "influencers" and these are: Sun, Moon, Mercury, Venus, Mars, Jupiter, Saturn, Uranus, Neptune and Pluto, as well as the North and South Nodes of the Moon - Rahu and Ketu.

SUN

The ultimate deity in our little piece of this cosmos is the Sun. The Sun is the father of everything, the central body around which all others revolve. Its shine is the essence, the light, the life in us, and the energy source for photosynthesis, which is the basic metabolic process for plants and even for animals. We are all eukaryotes after all. Without the Sun, we are not able to exist. This is also the first god in any early religion and the founder of the yearly calendar because we have the spring and autumnal equinoxes, and the summer and winter solstices. Around those four points in time, all of our rituals were created and worshiped throughout the existence of humankind. Nothing else is so powerful and nothing else can create or destroy us like the Sun.

Its qualities are: center, masculine, warm and dry, royalty, generosity, responsibility, light, warmth, vitality, power, honor, glory, reputation, authority, healthy ego, stability, maturity, calm enthusiasm, goodness. If it's placed in an unfavorable position and in tense aspects with other planets, or points on the chart, it can result in: vanity, arrogance, narcissism, snobbism and so on.

The Sun, forming a beneficial aspect with the other planets, will always give the characteristics of someone who doesn't know about mean behavior, a person with classy manners, with good judgment, and a natural born leader. Its negative planetary aspects will portray a person who is pretentious, egoist, or untrustworthy; someone who ruins order or life itself.

The Sun is the king, a middle-aged man, rich, or in other terms, a very successful man. This star also represents the day of Sunday, the lion, cats in general, bees, royal and golden colors, castles, decorations, gold, glitter, expensive jewelry, blond hair in females, a man who loses his hair when it comes to males, France and all royal families. It is the vision and therefore symbolized with eyes. In male charts, it is mainly the right eye, in female charts – the left one. In the terms of medical astrology, the Sun is the heart, the spine and the bone marrow, vitamin D, and many claim that it is also vitamin A; all crucially important parts of body.

In the terms of music, according to Pythagorean ideas, this is the sound "do".

The conjunction of the Sun and Moon, and their placement close to the North or the South Nodes of the Moon and some fixed stars like the Pleiades, Hyades or Praesepe can show blindness. Positive aspects with the Moon bring unity between the will and emotions, and good relationships between parents. Negative aspects show the internal war between the masculine and feminine, between the father and mother in us, and metabolic turmoil.

If Mercury, or any other planet, is placed too close with the Sun, then it is considered as burnt, so in this case, reasoning is damaged by ego. In the other case, when Mercury is positioned a bit further, this describes a person with great intelligence and someone prone to leadership. Venus with the Sun in positive aspects will show an admirer of beauty and good manners. However, the opposite will indicate problems between emotions and pleasure on one, and ego pretensions on the other side. Mars and the Sun together in positive combinations will show courage and power, but in the negative terms, this is someone prone to conflicts and agitation.

The Sun and Jupiter point to the greatest ruler, the most spiritual teacher, genuine guru, but on the negative side this is someone who is gaining weight too fast, and someone who fights authority, creates obstacles, squanders money or other resources, and leads a shameful life. With Saturn, the Sun can represent a reputation earned by hard work and dedication, gains of properties and knowledge. In negative terms, this is the curse of the ancestors, the mark of trouble, of problems with the father or a fatherly figure, and a heavy burden to carry throughout the whole life.

Uranus and the Sun can form unusual psychology in a person and depending on the aspects, this can be a genius when it comes to scientific or technological breakthroughs, but it can also be someone with bipolar disorder or the plain "slave of fashion trends". With Neptune, the Sun gives the gift of art, especially poetry, knowledge of chemistry and biology, but the negative side can be shown as an inclination toward illusions of all sorts. With Pluto, this is the spirit with demonic powers which can create the highest good, as well as the lowest of the low.

MOON

Lady Luna is the mother. Yes, the Earth is our real mother, but when it comes to the projection of celestial bodies someone had to take the role of the mother and having in mind that the Moon depends on the Sun reflecting its light on us during the night, Lady Luna is perceived as the dark side of the light in us. This is not necessarily bad, but opposite to order and masculine rules.

The motion of the Moon had been the basis of counting days, or nights, and creating "months" known as the lunar calendar. The Moon needs around 28 days to complete its circle and this is the center point of the small cycle in us in comparison to the "big" cycle based on the motion of the Sun.

Its qualities are: cold and moist, reflects the light, feminine, distanced, moody, responsive toward outer stimulation, psyche, strong fantasy, dependence, softness, wonderings, changes, suggestible, subjective. And all of these traits could become positive, negative or even both at the same time.

The Moon is the day of Monday, the mother in general, mother holding a baby, baby, people in general, like a nation, women, middle-aged women, sea, water, lake, night, coldness, water retention, water overflow. The Moon represents everything soft and with big eyes, fish and water creatures, wolves, dogs, slimy insects, blue, silver and even white colors, pearls, isolated places, mirrors, Holland and USA too, lighter and softer hair and skin, left eye in the male chart, right eye in the female chart.

In medical terms, the Moon rules the stomach, breasts, and womb, and when the woman is pregnant, the "full womb". It regulates the flow of water in our bodies and the lymph system. Together with Venus, this is mother's milk in female charts and it's the quality of sperm in male charts. It can be any of the vitamins coming from the B complex and in music, it's traditionally considered to be the note "Fa".

Too close to the Sun or in square or opposition with it, the Moon is dried out. Emotions have been burnt for the sake of the ego, survival or due to bad psychological "inheritance" coming from parents or parental figures. The good aspects are softening the will and advancing in life in accordance with feelings, not just logic.

Mercury and the Moon are two very odd friends if they make mutual aspects. In opposition or square, those two celestial bodies imply the liar or the cheater, or deceiver. If this is not the case, the person's feelings and thoughts are harmonized and well guided. Good aspects with Venus lead to delicate and elegant tastes, enjoyment in romance and food, while the opposite brings some sort of "soap opera" in the native's life because emotions and sense of pleasure differ. So when I know that I shouldn't eat that cake or I shouldn't seduce that married man but I can't resist, then the whole drama is born and this can lead to some spectacular resolutions. Looking on this from the brighter side, this is how literature was born and is created today...and how it will continue to be created.

The Moon and Mars are very special when coupled. Negatively speaking, Mars destroys the Moon, people become senseless, especially women, cruel and extremely aggressive in some cases. It can also show pain, injuries, and surgical interventions. On the positive side, Mars can give the Moon persistence and tenacity to go through most difficult tests in life. Jupiter is all about gaining weight with the Moon, water plus fat, but it can also describe the purity of the mind and the soul.

Saturn and the Moon are performing great when positioned in auspicious types of aspects. Discipline is above feelings and the person is ready to suffer or to reshape its soul and body to achieve success. Negatively, this is loneliness, long, chronic diseases, troubles with older feminine figures in life, especially mother or grandmother. With Uranus, it can point toward magnificent and extraordinary ideas or plain madness. Although the aspects with Neptune can look similar, in this case, the person can be an exquisite chemist, doctor, poet or saint, or on the other side, the dark side of the Moon, the person can be a drug addict, someone lost in the world of inner illusions and a skilled cheater.

Pluto and the Moon? Resurrection, the hardest tests for the body, the edge of losing the soul, "I just came from hell" type of thinking, type of smile, type of revenge.

MERCURY

The mind, logic, logistics, operative memory, trickster, Jack of all trade and master of none, "trust me, I'm an engineer" type of showing off. "He" can "she" and "she" can return to "he" or the ultimate "it". Mercury is known as the messenger of the gods and it goes wherever no god or no man would even step. He or she is cold and dry and never further than 27 degrees from the Sun, which implies that logic is never apart from ego.

It represents communication, trading, short travel, marketing, streets, neighborhoods, hallways, markets, schools, offices, journalism, rumors, gossips, often "right to the point" references and information, healing, health and herbalism, nutrition, wheat, grass, seeds, nuts, vitamin C, small intestine, lungs, brain, nervous system, birds, insects in general, small animals; you can find Mercury everywhere. Wednesday is his day. In music, this is the tone "Mi" and in education, this is something you can apply in real life right now, a simple calculation, but very useful every time. The color orange, but it can change from honey to chestnut shades, also all pastel colors and shades of autumn leaves and fruits. From Belgium to Tunisia, from Brazil to Greece, you'll find him in many countries as the main ruler.

Mercury in good aspect with Venus is the skilled lover, sweet talker, and smooth operator. In approaching square or in a negative type of conjunction this couple points clearly toward a cheater or someone very unreliable, especially in a committed love relationship. This can also be the sign of rude or insolent language or even person's inner desires can look like this. With Mars, Mercury can lead someone toward enormous success in engineering professions, due to their mutual "fast thinker and skilled worker" symbiosis. In negative aspects, this is the sign of a very rude person, passive-aggressive, someone who had been beaten as a child and now beats others, problems with hands, palms, lungs, intestines.

Jupiter and Mercury's combination is the match made in heaven when paired properly by astrological aspects. Jupiter directs the soul toward the greatest heights of human achievements, purity of intentions and spirituality, while Mercury organizes the mind to be disciplined and fast when it comes to implementation of the noble Jupiter's teachings. The other way around is called total chaos of the mind. If you don't know exactly what this means, try to imagine an attempt to trade with God during meditation, and then try walking down the street with your eyes closed and your thoughts directed toward heavens. Some people can live like this, but not for too long, if someone else is not taking care of them all the time.

Saturn and Mercury together in the auspicious positions is the sign of a great mathematician, respectable and stable thinking and well spoken, especially as this person gets older. On the negative side, this is a problem with the speech or tongue, fear of speaking and expressing, loneliness when it comes to ideas and self-promotion and mind blocks.

Mercury and Uranus are known as the main trait of electricians, astrologers, geniuses and mad people. This is the basic model for electricity, in mind, in a body, in ideas. The conjunction of those two fast and furious celestial bodies frequently implies autoimmune diseases or neurological problems, or most likely both. In good aspects, this is the image of a spotless mind, but when bad times activate bad aspects of them, this is the clear danger of electrical stroke whether it comes from inside or outside sources. In those particular cases some medical diagnostic tools, like ultrasound or X-rays exams can damage such native.

A quality tarot card reader is known as someone with trines or sextiles between Neptune and Mercury. The same goes for a guitar player and if you add Venus to this formula, then you get the perfect musician, no matter what instrument is involved. Neptune is here to inspire, while Mercury serves to channel the message of intuition. If aspects between them are tense, this is the sign of a liar, cheater, or at least, messy speaker. Pluto and Mercury are indicating someone with heightened drama in communication or during usual daily obligations. This can also be the poisonous speech, but if positive, the person with this aspect can heal with just loud praying.

VENUS

She is pleasure itself. Is this good? Not necessarily, because Venus has the longstanding reputation of someone who challenged the almighty God or the Supreme Power or Energy (choose whatever you like the best) and was punished for her ideas and deeds. In western astrology, Venus is considered as a female planet, but traditional views look at "her" like Lucifer, the light bearer, someone who was most beautiful, skilled and intelligent among all angels. Those characteristics slowly, but surely led him to believe that he can be better than the God (Sun) itself and in the end, he was punished by being expelled to the underworld. Vedic myth concerning Venus differ somewhat, but the conclusion is the same. You will be punished if you start imagining your greatness greater than the Supreme Greatness. Vanity can be hell sometimes.

Venus is beauty, harmony, elegance, desire for material security, dancing school, wardrobe, court of law, garden, flowers, jewelry, shiny stones, fashion, sweets, especially chocolates, perfumes, assessors, romance, romantic literature, poetry, music, dancing, sheep, all small and soft animals. She is cold and moist by nature and her colors are blue, green, turquoise and even white. Her day is Friday. Her lands are Austria, Switzerland, Canada, China, Argentina and most of all, she loves beauty through an order.

Her organs are the throat, lower jaw, thyroid gland, neck, skin, and kidneys. She regulates the blood pressure and the levels of copper in blood. And her favorite sports, besides noble types of joy, like ballroom dancing, are qigong or yoga, disciplines known for their power of balancing and harmonizing inner energies. She is the queen of vitamin E, something necessary for the beauty of the skin.

Venus is "La", of course.

With Mars, this is the basic story of love, romantic pursuing and carnal passion. Negative aspects between them can cause havoc in a person's life, but on the brighter side, this is how art was founded in the first place. Jupiter and Venus are true love and devotion for spiritual teachings and, also, true love and devotion toward a good and useful sugar daddy, while on the negative side this is the sign that the person is not capable to budget for expenses or expenses tend to build up no matter what other safety actions are previously taken.

Saturn and Venus mean stability and tradition if positioned fine. However, on the other side, this is life without love, without true love, frustration, and coldness. Great for sculptors, horrible for lovers. Uranus and Venus usually meet through social media, airplanes or any other unusual place and time. There is the spark, there is the fire and there is one big nothing after. Disappointment usually lasts the longest, but the mistakes tend to be repeated in the case that the person has negative aspects between those two planets. In a positive way, this is the sign of exclusive taste, unusual, but lasting love with the pilot, astronaut, and scientist and so on.

Astonishing, gorgeous, wonderfully magical can be the voice of Venus when joined with Neptune. This is the fairy, the angel, the purest of the pure, the softest of the soft and the sweetest of all sweet things in this realm. But, when those two are in the tense aspects, this is the cheater of all cheaters, carrier of venereal diseases, or it can be shown as various missionaries trying to buy your soul using all sorts of manipulative psychological techniques. And this is, also, passion toward alcohol and frequently illegal substances. Venus and Pluto is the story of the Lord of the Underworld and his bride. Being positive or negative, this type of aspect always reminds us that there is a price we have to pay. The greater the pleasure – the greater the price will be.

MARS

He is our drive for life, for sex, for action. He is a warrior in every one of us. Masculine, his nature is hot and dry, his color is red, naturally and he is all about breakthroughs, "cut and enter" philosophies, so he can also be an expert when it comes to surgery. Of course, he is courageous, open, truthful and direct. He loves to reside in fighting places like dojos and open grounds too. Swords, guns, machines, advancing through deserts, through jungles, through mountains, there is always a war going on, and something and someone has to be conquered. Mars is the enemy to every other planet, except Venus. Her softness and femininity are his final defeat, but he can't resist her and he won't be able to resist her until the time runs out in this universe.

When negatively positioned or aspected with other celestial bodies, he is so hard to handle, heavy when it comes to polemics; annoying, destructive, full of injuries, verbal or physical fights with no particular reason or outcome, psychopath, murderer, dog or war; he can be everything.

His sound is "So", his vitamin K. He rules Tuesday, and in the terms of medical astrology he is the nose, the muscles, genitals, blood, and controls the levels of iron or red blood cells directly. His animals are all aggressive animals, no matter how small or big they are, especially males in animal species. Countries under his heavenly government are Germany, Japan, Israel, Syria, and Korea.

With Jupiter, he can become a warrior priest, military doctor, dignified expert, but when their aspects are negative this is the sign of agitator, manipulator, spitfire type of guy, always in conflicts with authorities, but it can be also beneficial for entrepreneurs if they manage to get "the rules of the game". His association with Saturn brings exceptional strength and discipline, gaining the fortune in the second part of life and longevity. However, if positioned in negative aspects, this is traditionally considered to be the hardest planetary aspect there is in the whole science of astrology. World wars are starting with this seal in heavens, and personal lives are filled with such hard challenges which can extend beyond human imagination. Car accidents, permanent disabilities, killing someone out of duty, accidentally killing someone, tough decisions, ruined happiness for the rest of a person's life.

Mars and Uranus bring a dash of gunpowder, electricity followed with an explosion. Great for engineering, technical breakthroughs, thinking out of the box, sudden turnarounds, but for a better solution. Negatively positioned, those two planets indicate strongly the danger of car accidents, electric shock, sudden attack, sexual deviations and aggression, criminal mind and similar fast and furious events and people. Neptune can bring magnificent insights regarding sailing, astrophysics, higher mathematics, hydraulics, and pneumatics. This aspect also gives great intuition when it comes to taking action and not taking action, proper place, and proper moment to strike or to pull back. Their negative traits bring the worst out of the person. This is the cheater, deceiver, criminal type of guy ready to do anything low to get what he needs. It also indicates alcoholic psyche, substances abuse, no matter whether those substances are legal or illegal.

Pluto and Mars fall under the special category because the position of Pluto has to be prominently placed in the chart to be active. But this is all about highest drama there is, childhood trauma which can't be healed followed by great inner transformation. Good aspects indicate enormous strength, the power to bare an unbearable, explosive, but creative mind. While the bad aspect shows sudden danger, sudden death, sudden victory.

JUPITER

This planet is a world of its own. Jupiter is almost like a little Sun in our system, with twelve satellites and the power to protect us from the outer cosmic bodies. He is all about expansion, education, broader views, religious teachings, long distance traveling, sailing over the open seas, archery, hunting, honor, noble tradition, synthesis of knowledge, law, and order, goodness, generosity. His day is Thursday, he is hot and moist and his color is bright yellow, but it can also be a bit darker, like saffron. Remember Buddhists or Hindi priests in their yellow or orange robes? This is the symbol for Jupiter.

In the terms of medical astrology, Jupiter is fat tissue and brain together with Mercury, liver and gallbladder, thighs, and buttocks, vitamin R. His animal is a horse or an elephant, but wild and free animals like deer or eagles all fall into his kingdom. It also loves to reside in woods and open spaces. His lands are Australia, Chile, South Africa, North Africa, Portugal, Scandinavia. According to Pythagoras's teachings, his sound is "Ti".

Of course, there are negative traits related to this planet; this is the main rule of the life itself. Jupiter can also gain weight fast, he can become overwhelming, endlessly unrestrained, vain, boring, manipulative and with a dirty mind or emotions. People often blame Saturn for their obstacles, and especially health problems. But at the same time, they tend to forget that no other planet can strike you so hard and fast with such expansion as Jupiter can do it.

In association with Saturn, this planet gives an exceptional and structured type of thinking and planning, achieving properties and wealth in general terms. These are constructive and systematic methods in business, agriculture, governmental tasks and in education. Those types of positive aspects are extremely significant in personal horoscopes, and astrologers in general tend to assume that all founders of main religions, like Buddha, Jesus, and Mohammed, had this aspect prominent in their natal charts. Negatively placed, energy exchanged between Saturn and Jupiter can lead to the loss of position or reputation, troubles with court cases and law, tendency for self-destruction, persecution, and serious problems for the father or grandfather of the person.

When you think about lottery gains, you have to associate Jupiter with Uranus in the heavenly formula for sudden success. This is also the image of the eccentric mind, unconventional thoughts, and often people's heroes during the times of war, and in some cases genius. Negative traits of this aspect are indicating a crazy person, someone who squanders his talent for worthless inventions, sudden losses, aggressive atheism, great problems caused by educated people.

Jupiter with Neptune is all about spirituality and the highest moral standards one person can acquire through life. This is the symbol for the accomplished saint who became the true role model for the masses, the teacher, and the avatar. A person with this aspect is not capable of distinguishing others related to their social levels, castes, races. The same person is deeply emotionally involved with suffering and resolving all problems regarding the suffering of people, animals, plants, the Earth itself. The negative side of this aspect can also show its grandiose or the wideness of evil because the person can become involved in a cult. This is the clear sign of someone who is the member or the leader of the religious sect, but political parties can be in play here also. Manipulation and humiliating perpetration, very twisted and often sick crimes are all present with this aspect.

Pluto with Jupiter can show the depthless quality of the mind. So-called "zeroing" when understanding is at its highest level that it negates itself. Singularity of spiritual thoughts, fast and strong transformation, resurrection, transmutation. Negative aspects between those two planets indicate horrible suffering due to religious beliefs, egoism and ecstasy, triumph through total destruction, victory through loss and vice versa.

SATURN

This is probably the most feared planet in the whole Solar system. It's known as the "Ring Pass Not" because planet Saturn with its recognizable rings was considered to be the border guardian of our sky and on the other side the mystery of the spiritual realm begins.

This celestial body is directly related to the flow of time, discipline, persistence, durability, seriousness, responsibility, reasoning, but it also governs properties, stones, especially precious pieces, old castles, graveyards, crypts, basements, top of the mountains, hard terrains in general, goats, hogs, mice, all small, but strong animals are his favorite pets, because they never give up.

Bulgaria, Tibet, India, Russia, Ethiopia, Iran, these are the countries marked by Saturn. His nature is cold and dry and it rules during the Saturdays. Prominent colors are black, of course, ashy shades, even purple or ultraviolet in rare cases. In the terms of medical part of astrology, this planet represents the bones, teeth and knees, skeletal system and our ability to stand upright. And it is also vitamin D, crucially important for the health of the bones. His sound is "Re" and he is portrayed as the old skinny man with prominent nose and ears.

The negative side of Saturn is a life full of obstacles, hunger, poverty, chronic diseases, deadly illnesses, freezing cold, endless waiting for things to get better, lack of resources, lack of love, lack of everything. The extreme pressure which can break or destroy many, but from exceptional ones Saturn makes exquisite jewels. Its symbol is the diamond because this is just the piece of coal which had to go through enormous pressures and temperature changes to become the hardest one and the most beautiful, most precious clear stone.

Together with Uranus, Saturn tends to preach about the ideas of socialism, communism, revolutions, how poor and insignificant rise against rich and royals to establish the new kingdom of equality. This usually happens through blood and new types of oppression. This can also indicate new ideas regarding science with results acquired through long and laborious research work. The negative side shows a longing for authority with unclear causes or outcomes, drastic behavior, damaged neurology and psyche, anarchism, eccentricity, problems with authorities or with the law.

Neptune and Saturn are good companions when it comes to the oil and gas industry, all things related to mining, especially underwater drilling, and excavations. This is also the sign of someone who can perceive the geometry of space or spaces together in the mind or in the speculative realms of geometry. Good for "serious" types of music, old instruments, legends, myths and ancestral teachings. It can lead some people to become the channel between the world of the dead and the world of the living. Negatively this aspect describes the liar, someone who doesn't just lie but twists the truth, especially in the political sense. Manipulation over masses through news or education, strange diseases, epidemics, death by stifling, nicotine or any other source of smoking addiction, asthma, cataracts.

Saturn and Pluto are considered to be the sign of an ancestral curse, black magic, dead bodies, massive destruction, investigation, archeology, forensics, sadism, ascetics. There are really no just good or just bad aspects between those two planets. Everything related to them is truly related to the greatest depths of our beings, the essence of the soul, reaching for the demon and dancing with him.

And this is the moment when we have exited the traditional heavens and discovered the new planets. Their influence wasn't so prominent before their discoveries, but from the point in time when we became aware of them, they incorporated into our lives and took the meanings and symbolism of our inventions too.

Planets outside the traditional astrology are mainly considered as the indicators of collective and social trends. They are more important for the political, cultural or technological changes than personal ones, but in some cases, when those planets make the direct aspects with traditional celestial bodies, then they can play major roles in the life of the native.

URANUS

Everything is sudden and everything is unusual when it comes to this planet. The gift of discoveries, technological breakthroughs, reforms of society and many more traits belong to Uranus. He can be the visionary, although his looks show someone coming from the plain origin. Newness through revolution is his signature. On the negative side, this is a person who is prone to collective trends and thought patterns, a destroyer of an aristocracy, the announcer of catastrophes and triumphs. Prometheus is his real name, for better and for worse. He rules over electricity, x-rays and IT technologies. And regarding traditional astrology, Uranus is seen as the "higher octave" of the planet Mercury. You can say freely – Mercury on steroids. Color is light blue, silver, any metallic shade.

In good planetary aspects with Neptune, this planet shows global trends, gifted mystics, faith, esoteric sciences, ideals of love and humanity, enthusiasm, heavenly music. Negative aspects bring out the fight against the norms and conventions, fall of idols and teachings, political fallacies, sexual disorders and adventurism which can lead to serious danger.

Pluto and Uranus together are never even close to the image of a harmless couple. This is the electricity combined with nuclear power, magicians, yogis, secret medicine, energy healing, scalar waves, tunneling through dimensions, mystical cults, poisoning, occult, psychiatrists, manias in all positive or negative sense of those words, although in those cases there is nothing even close to being considered as pure "positive" or "negative". It's just amazing in its creativity or destruction.

NEPTUNE

The god of the sea…of illusion. Traditionally seen as the higher octave of the planet Venus and therefore considered as something beyond beautiful, inspirational, delicate beyond perception, magically and sparkling rhythmical, glitter not gold. He also possesses the gift of demonic intuition, the gift of abstract thinking, higher philosophy related to natural sciences, diving into the depths of the sea, of the sky, cosmos, cells, biochemical processes. On the negative side, and yes, Neptune has a negative side as all other planets, this is the generic model of a liar, deceiver, a fraud, fake preacher, fake love, fake faith, fake education. It also had the tendency toward hoaxes, however, it's hard to fight with him. How can you fight fog? When and if got caught, he plays confused. All drugs are here, legal or illegal, all smoking tendencies, bacterial infections, poisoned water, poisoned air.

With any other planet Neptune achieves the miraculous initial success, enchantment and romance follow and then everything ends with disappointment, shame, dishonor, and blasphemy. Together with

Pluto, this is poison, extremely high potency poison. Everything is ruined and covered with an indelible layer of pure venom which will last forever, like the consequence of nuclear explosion. In positive aspects, this is the sign of greatest mystic there is, a magician or someone who is dancing on the edge of divine devotion and total craziness.

PLUTO

The god of the underworld, many call him "fatum". He is the blackest of all black in color, he is the husband of the most beautiful woman and he rules over corpses. Without him, and her, the outer world can't be awakened, can't bloom and reproduce. On our ancestors, we all stand, from the roots we all grow. He is our origin, he is a resurrection, and he will be the end. Small, but dangerous like the energy in the single atom, like a nucleus, like nuclear. Pluto is considered to be the higher octave of the planet Mars and you can come pretty close to the right characteristics of this planet if you imagine it as the Mars with a genius mind and weapons powerful beyond anything else in the Universe...or perhaps Multiverse.

Pluto won't show its powers in any chart. It has to be positioned in angular houses (first, fourth, seventh and tenth) or to make a significant aspect with other planets. In those cases, you can see its powers, but even if you do, you'll wish you didn't.

NORTH AND SOUTH NODES OF THE

MOON

North Node of the Moon is known as the Dragon's head and the South Node of the Moon is known as the Dragon's tail and those are traditional western names for the two calculative points in the sky. In Vedic astrology, those points are known as Rahu and Ketu and further on in this text, they will be addressed by those names, because this is widely spread all over the astrological world.

Rahu, as the North Node, and Ketu, as the South Node, are two opposite points in the chart and these points are the markers where the path of the Moon is crossing the ecliptic belt. These are not celestial bodies and they are always exactly 180 degrees apart from each other.

Myths associate Rahu as the head without the body, while Ketu is the body without the head. Rahu is something we have to process and learn during this current life, while Ketu is something we have already mastered through many of our lives, or in the previous life, which is important for this life in the terms of karma. Of course, if you believe in karma.

Those points tend to become very powerful when they are joined with planets in natal charts and they are capable of creating real havoc or powerful blessing, depending on other planetary aspects, and coming solar and lunar eclipses regarding transits.

Eclipses happen due to the fact that Sun and Moon are together on one of those two points or they are in opposition on the Rahu-Ketu axis. They bring changes; they take some things, issues, ideas or people we no longer need from us and present us with new events, people, issues, and ideas, whether we want this to happen or not. This is the nature of life, constant changes and growth through those changes.

Eclipses happening on the natal Sun can indicate a new direction in life, the danger for the father, while the eclipsed Moon can represent the danger for the mother or the soul of the native. Venus associated with Nodes will always bring unresolved issues into your love life and great instability with women, while similar can be applied for Mars, but in the terms of activity, men, enthusiasm. When the Nodes are placed together with Jupiter, a person will always seek higher knowledge, transform and adopt new teachings. With Saturn and Nodes joined in the natal chart, a person will feel cursed until the hard lessons about life, health, career, and discipline are mastered completely.

Association between Uranus, Neptune, and Pluto with Rahu or Ketu will always point in the direction of scientific, artistic or technological breakthroughs and those people will certainly have to go through many challenges, but at the same time, they will feel the strong, driving force to carry on and they don't give up on their dreams.

HOW TO READ THE

ASTROLOGICAL CHART

Simply put, an astrological chart is the projection of the sky on the Earth's plane. Of course, that the Earth is not a plane, but this is not the question here because we approximate the image of the sky onto ourselves as if we were the center of the world. And if we "catch" the image of the sky at the same moment we were born, then we have the "natal chart". The same is applicable for the charts of the animals, buildings, companies, business deals, events like weddings, receptions and anything you can think of. These are all natal charts and they all describe the potential for good and bad events, which can happen further on, depending on some other factors.

The main one of those "other factors" are planetary transits. They are the most important fact in western astrology; while the Vedic school favors divisional charts, which is an arrangement of the planets and sensitive points in the chart calculated through some geometrical and mathematical rules. However, we will discuss the western or tropical school of astrology here. To avoid confusion, you should know that Vedic or sidereal astrology deals with sidereal positions of the planets in the sky, while western astrology deals with tropical positions or the projection of planets on the Earth's plane. In simple words, for example, the first day of spring is March 21st. We know this because day and night are equal and this is called the spring equinox. The Sun enters into the sign of Aries and the new cycle begins. You know that this is the equinox; you know that spring is here, but if you go to the observatory and look at the Sun through a telescope, you will see that Sun is still in the constellation of Pisces. This "effect" is happening due to the precession of the equinoxes; however, for now this concept is beyond the basics of astrology.

The most important thing you have to know is that both astrological schools are right, they have their precise prediction systems, which differ, but they both work. The quality of the prediction depends on the quality of chosen astrologer, not the school which is selected for the reading.

Let's get back to planetary transits. This is the term which describes the image of the current or upcoming planetary arrangement in the sky. If you, for instance, overlap the transit chart over your natal chart, you will be able to see the areas where you are challenged, blessed, where can you grow, in what to invest, from what or who to beware and so on. Sometimes the warning signs are extremely obvious if you know how to read those two sets of planetary arrangements together.

The same applies to your partner's charts, whether they can show the development and the outcome of love, business or any other relationship. All you need to do is to overlap those two charts and to read mutual aspects that the planets make.

GENERAL ASTROLOGY RULES

First, you have to know the meaning of each planet and the meaning of each astrological sign. Then you have to know the basic aspects planets make together.

The chart in the western astrology style is presented as a circle divided into 12 parts, each one representing astrological houses. The most important points are the Ascendant – Descendant (Asc-Dsc) line, which is a horizontal line in the chart and the Medium Coeli – Imum Coeli (MC-IC) line, which is showing the highest and the lowest points of your chart. Those are four of the most important points you have to pay attention to. Asc is your rising sign, describing just you. Dsc is how you deal with your love, business or any other partner and how you project yourself into the world. IC is your origin, while MC is your highest accomplishment.

A circle with the cross in it, it is so simple, and the whole life in it.

The image of your natal chart will look like this circle, but with the snapshot of the planetary arrangements at the moment you were born. This snapshot holds the potentials which will develop to a greater or a lesser degree, depending on upcoming planetary transits during your life. Whether those potentials and life's events are good or bad, you will know by reading the aspects the planets make.

PLANETARY ASPECTS

Whenever celestial body moves through the heavens, it creates a motion, therefore frequency, and therefore sound. Any relation between celestial bodies creates a mutual aspect and all together they make the music of the spheres. However, the aspects considered as the most important in astrology are conjunction, sextile, square, trine and opposition.

Conjunction happens when the two planets are placed close to each other so their influences are mixed. If there are three or more planets involved, then this is called stellium. Are the planets forming conjunction or stellium? This depends on their orbs of influences. Bigger bodies have greater orbs and for the Sun, Moon, Jupiter, and Saturn, this can extend to 15 degrees because they are big planets with great strength. Also, depending on the planets involved, conjunction can be considered as good or bad.

Sextile is formed between planets when they form the 60-degree angle between them looking from the center point of an astrological circle or a chart. Generally speaking, this is a good aspect and suggests that planets are active and can result in a positive outcome.

Square happens when two planets form a 90-degree angle in the chart and squares are often perceived as bad aspects because they can bring very challenging situations in our lives. But, at the same time, they force us to change and to grow in attempts to overcome or resolve our problems.

Trine is seen as the exceptionally auspicious aspect and it happens when two planets form a 120-degree angle between them. Although beneficial, trines can sometimes produce a lazy attitude, so there is really nothing just black and white going on in the sky.

An opposition is another "bad" aspect because two celestial bodies are forming 180-degrees angle and they are directly opposing each other. This is challenging too, causing open war between opposite sides, frictional, but at the same time, it provokes the search for a better option or solution.

ZODIAC SIGNS AND HOUSES

Now that we have learned the general meaning of planets and aspects in the chart, we should take the closer look at the astrological signs and houses. As you already know, the horoscope is divided into four sectors (remember the cross in the circle?) and twelve "houses" or main areas of life. In Vedic astrology, those houses are equal. Each one extends to 30 degrees. However, in the western school, this is not the case, because the geometry of the point on Earth where you were born, for instance, is calculated through various systems. This is something which is beyond the basics, but you should know that today, Placidus house system is mostly used and it shows the best results, except in the case that person was born in the areas of polar circles.

The main rule of astrology is that each Zodiac sign has the meaning of the same house. Translated, this rule can be easily explained looking at the signs. Aries is the first sign in the Zodiac belt, so the first house of any horoscope has the general meaning of the sign of Aries; the second house has the meaning of Taurus and so on until we reach to the Pisces or twelfth house.

For instance, you can be born in the sign of Gemini and this means that you were born between the 21st of May until 20th of June. However, if you were born, let's say, during the afternoon hours, your rising sign or your Ascendant could be placed in the sign of Scorpio. This is just an example; we will have to know the exact time to see where the Ascendant is placed.

Now, you have your natal Sun in Gemini, but your rising sign is Scorpio. This means that your first house is placed in the sign of Scorpio, but at the same time, this means that you will have all the traits of Aries (first house) through the characteristics of Scorpio. In this case, also, the Sun is placed in Gemini, but in the eighth house of the horoscope, which again carries the symbolism of the sign of Scorpio. Add to this mix the position of your natal Moon and you will have the basic understanding of your character and appearance.

It can sound a bit complicated for an absolute beginner, but in time and with the little practice, you will start using those "double" systems, not even thinking about them while applying the rules.

Right now, have in mind that Hor, Horus or Hrs is the son of the god of time and this word can be found in many Indo-European languages and also in Egypt. Horoscope was the name for the priest who controls the measuring of the time. "Horos-scopein" means literally the clock watcher. Horoscope is all about the flow of time through the certain place, but is this the driving force through entire Universe?

Let's find out.

ARIES

Sun transits through Aries from the 21st of March until the 21st of April and during this period of time, the Sun increases its power rapidly, nature is awakening and suddenly we feel the urge to take action.

The sign of Aries or the first house in the chart is all about me, ego, will. The ruler of this sign is the planet Mars, which is diurnal (through daytime), this is also the male sign, the element is fire and the color is red. Aries is the cardinal sign and planet Mars rules Tuesday. Countries under this sign are Germany, Japan, Israel, Syria, Poland.

Aries is the image of the perfect soldier. He is strong, determined, a patriot, skilled in the art of war. He is also fast, with a rudimentary type of will, one-sided in his thinking, but honest and often naïve. With the strong constitution and proper training – he is extremely dangerous. His favorite places are open spaces for sporting or martial arts activities, stadiums, city centers, all tall and new buildings made of steel and glass.

His feelings are fiery, passionate, easily affected, always above reasoning. His commitment to love can last for a very short or very long time, depending on the levels of passion he receives from his partner. In business, he needs some time to get the "rules of the game", but when he incorporates them then the breakthroughs are made. As a worker, he is very loyal, but tends to create tremendous stress and needs the time for relaxing after.

His best professions are related to sports, military, engineering, metallurgy, surgeries and any other type of duty where responsibility, clear line of command, order, and activity are necessary. He loves uniforms of any sort, no matter whether those uniforms are of the military and medical nature. He will equally enjoy the "uniform" of his favorite sports club, or him being dressed as a butcher, electrician, plumber or any other profession he is in.

There is no need to suppress this grandiose energy or Martian rage, especially when it comes to children born in the sing of the Ram. It's better to channel it through sports and activities in nature. Aries natives need to eat healthily, drink a lot of pure water and to spend their time in open spaces under the Sun. They should keep out of the stale atmosphere, small spaces, and boring environments.

Young women tend to be insecure because they are uncertain about the levels of their energy. They can be perceived as too strong and this ruins their chances for romance. And romance they want, indeed, like we all do. In this case, they feel better in groups and for them, and all other younger Aries natives, it's imperative to use the powerful inner drive creatively, because if they don't - they will tend to become members or even the leaders of delinquency groups.

Marriage for Aries people happens early and if their partner is calm in nature or prone to more feminine energies, this union will last for a lifetime because they need someone to be their safe fortress when they come back home. They are faithful because they are unable to lie and even if they fall in love beside their official partner, they will break this affair pretty quickly or they will divorce fast and remarry even faster. The sign of Ram is about honesty, even when it's based on naivety; about newness and rebirth. Strong outside, but very soft inside, the Ram is brave, interested in everything around him and careless like a baby.

The natives are not insensitive, as others could start to think; they are just bursting with energy and usually joy and precisely because they are so sensitive deep down inside, they cover their softness with the shield of sports, martial arts or membership of any organized group.

Sun exalts here in the sign of the Ram or in the first house of the horoscope because the Sun is the king and king just loves to show off leading his armies to war. This is the clear sign of very strong ego, self-sustaining type of thinking and living habits. In positive aspects with other planets, this is the characteristic of a psychologically strong native with a heightened sense of justice. However, when afflicted this Sun can show a tendency to become the dictator, he will certainly be inadequate when it comes to compromising and prone to quarreling, jealousy and simply unbearable. It can also indicate injuries of the eyes.

The Moon is seen as "too dried out" in this sign because the nature of the Moon is to be cold and moist and in those circumstances, the Moon is left on the hot and dry surface. A person with the Moon in the first house or placed in Aries will tend to have a short temper, sometimes brisk attitude and often be insensitive toward other's emotions. Injuries of the eyes (dry eyes) show in this case too, but together with the hurt feelings.

Mercury feels good wherever he resides, or at least he thinks so. This small planet of communication here doesn't know when to stop and words, words, words are spilled all around, often said in a rude manner or through an irritated tone. Agitator, a messenger in war, but good for sports, especially group sports like basketball, volleyball and similar activities.

Planet Venus is in detriment in the sign of Aries. This doesn't mean that she is losing her powers; it's simply the sign that she doesn't feel good here. Short hair, red hair, red lipstick, red clothes, sometimes sloppy and not so finely paired, sports shoes with the dress, elegant handbag with yoga pants, she can make great fashion designers cry out of sadness or a joy, depending on the positions of other planets. This is also the only position of Venus which indicates a turnaround in the game of love. Woman pursues a man, or in the case of male's horoscope, he waits to be pursued by a woman. For gay couples, this means that the one with dominant female's energy pursues the one with the dominant male's energy.

Mars is in his home here. Strong and powerful, but hard to handle. It also points into the direction of constant stress, even strokes, injuries of the head, especially the nose, redness in the face and body and often, scars. Blond and reddish blond, curly hair. Mars in Aries or in the first house rules the head - the skull (but without the lower jaw) and the hair.

Jupiter placed in the first house or in the sign of Aries shows joyous temperament, prone to weight gains, fatty cheeks and round eyes. An enthusiastic person, highly educated if other planetary positions are supportive and this is the image of the military priest or military doctor.

Saturn is in fall in Aries or in the first house. This indicates a very stubborn person, overwhelmed with life's changes. The danger of loss of hearing, injury to ears, problems with the upper teeth and even brain tumors. Stressful search for justice, for peace, for rest.

Uranus in Aries and also in the first house is the sudden explosion with long-lasting consequences. Unusual mind or methodology of thinking, "out of the box" solutions when Uranus is positively supported by the other planets, and a harsh and even crazy character in challenging positions. Use of the newest frequency types of technologies in engineering or as a weapon. Bipolar disorders, a pressure in the eyes, nervous breakdowns.

Neptune in Aries can be the true disaster. This is the planet of illusions, so in such dry theater of war operations, this planet is lost in alcohol and drugs. This can also point toward secret and popular "sports" among soldiers which include some sort of religious devotion mixed with drugs, most likely illegal ones. Generally, it can show problems with eyes, like cataracts, dementia, but also the talents for acting. In good aspects, this points toward hydraulics and pneumatics, new engineering technologies when it comes to water, oil or gases.

Pluto in Aries or in the first house is all about resurrection. Independent fanatic spirit, strong will and volcanic types of instincts. Demonic attraction and mad courage, black magic, fall, unique history.

TAURUS

The Sun transits through the sign of Taurus from the 21st of April until the 21st of May and during this time frame the Sun is stabilizing, everything in nature is ready for propagation. This is the time of quiet excitement, love, pleasure.

The sign of Taurus or the second house in the chart is all about mine, properties, belongings. The ruler of this sign is the planet Venus, which is here nocturnal (through nighttime) according to Ptolemy's Table of Essential Dignities; this is also the female sign, the element is the earth and the colors are brown and green. Taurus is the fixed sign and the planet Venus rules Friday. Countries under this sign are Ireland, Switzerland, Cuba, Tanzania, Cyprus.

Taurus is a female sign and that is why is easier to think of her as one very healthy and strong woman coming from the natural environment. She is slow and meticulous, but steady and she gets her work done. Someone might think that she is not so bright, but her slowness is far from being dumb. She knows the value of everything in every moment and this is why the sign of Bull is so important for monetary transactions.

She holds the keys to all rooms on her property and in every second she knows how much money her family possesses and where will expenses appear and how will the profits be made.

She is traditional and yes, she is the essence of value.

In medical terms, Taurus rules over the neck, thyroid gland, many hormones and lower jaw. Natives born in this sign tends to accumulate weight through life and if this is the case with women, many of them will have to starve their bodies to remain near the looks of a modern ideal of beauty. However, many of those women just give up and they enjoy this accumulation of everything, including fat.

Marriages last for a lifetime and many times love is being born out of the pure calculation, which is absolutely nothing bad in the eyes of one Taurus because substantial resources are the only guarantee for the happy ever after. How can we talk about love when I haven't seen your properties? How will I ever think of starting a family with you if you don't have enough money? What do you expect – to keep my future children hungry? These are all very realistic question one Taurus will think about even on the first date.

Children of this sign are peaceful and they desperately need the time spent outside in nature. You will raise them the best if you keep them playing on the meadow, in the woods, near the animals. And let them work all farmers' types of jobs or let them experiment in the kitchen. They won't all be involved in agriculture, but many of them will become the great biologists, especially botanists, builders, architects, exclusive cooks, animal trainers, veterinarians. But on the other side, this world of matter will make out of many of them respected bankers, investors, industrialists, high profile managers. Don't worry about their future, because they will be capable to raise their kingdom even if they don't possess a thing in the beginning.

The Sun generally feels good in the sign of Taurus or placed in the second house of the horoscope. This is all about incomes and all about earning money in style. However, profits are in most cases made through the land, farming, especially fruits and vegetables, although raising stock is also popular among these natives. Every business deal is checked first with parents, parental figures or a spouse. Tradition is important and respected through generations. Strong neck, strong voice.

The Moon just loves to be in Taurus. This is the place where the Moon exalts because it deals with security and family fortune. It's so easy to feel good when food is plenty, the land is fertile, stables are full of animals and rooms are full of children. Harmony and love. Big sensitive eyes, women tend to gain weight easily, especially in the second part of life, and there could be some problems with the thyroid gland. It's necessary for the person with any planet in this sign, especially the Moon, to walk bare feet on the ground.

Mercury is a bit slow here. It takes time to form the sentence, to think, to read. He doesn't even want to bother with those things when calculating profits and expenses are his favorite activities. Geometry is perhaps something too complicated to deal with, but when it comes to other mathematical areas like the stock market, Taurus Mercury can be invincible.

When placed well, this indicates that the person loves to sing those old witty folk songs or the native has a natural gift for hip-hop reciting. Nice incomes from several small sources.

Venus is the fairy queen here. She is the best looking girl in the whole county and perhaps even further. This is her kingdom and she feels good in her body, in her home, in her properties, and with her own money. In many cases, she has a magical voice and singing is her natural talent. When receiving some negative aspects, this Venus can behave a bit like a sugar baby. Over the course of years, as her fortune increases, her weight will increase too. There are so many cases when a woman with this position is famous in the world of entertainment, has everything, but starves deliberately because her body accumulates everything. She adores designer's pieces in fashion, elegant clothes and extremely expensive handbags, shoes, and jewelry.

Mars is in his sign of detriment in Taurus. He doesn't lose his power, but he feels lazy and defeated by the fullness of life. There are no wars to fight in the rich land of eternal spring. He is like the soldier on his days off, so he just lies on the ground, looking at the sky or checking if any of the village girls walk nearby. He is also the great chef here and he is known for his meals made out of meat. Royal nutrition, yes, he also gains weight easily, but his body is big and covered in muscles. He loves woods and he finds his talents through working as a carpenter or peasant here. In the second house of horoscope, Mars creates expenses, usually for the home and personal items, but still expenses.

Jupiter in Taurus or placed in the second house can bring fortune, but this will happen only if the native is honest, educated and well prepared. This planet behaves like the omen from heavens here, but only if the ground is prepared in advance. Methodical techniques in agriculture bring success and methodical thinking goes the long way with Jupiter in the house of incomes.

Saturn in Taurus can indicate poverty in a very shallow sense of understanding astrology. This is happening because the influences of Jupiter and Saturn are misunderstood. Jupiter is the fortune, but the fortune in a spiritual or educational sense, while

Saturn is the one to symbolize wealth in the terms of real, material properties. In this particular case the native can start poor and end rich, or the native can possess the ability to find cheap or to inherit something insignificant and turn it into a fortune. Great position for surface mining, archeology, sculpting, turning old peasant houses and farms into exclusive retreats. Good for banking also.

Uranus in Taurus is all about stock market changes, new agricultural technologies, disrupted currencies and economic crises. When Uranus is placed in the second house triggered by the other planetary transits it can create sudden gains or sudden losses of wealth.

Neptune in Taurus is all about trying to put down the heavens on the earth. In the positive context, this relates to art. A person is capable of making or singing heavenly music; this is innovation regarding sculpting and also amazing architecture. Someone might discover a geyser on the property, but on the negative side, this is extreme sensitivity toward chemicals and the danger of choking. Monetary gains through cheating.

Pluto in Taurus is great for forensics. This is all about digging bodies, digging knowledge, digging precious artifacts. It's also the demonic power of the Earth itself and some very weird ways of earning money while dancing on the edge of the law.

GEMINI

The Sun transits through the sign of Gemini from the 21st of May until the 20th of June and during this time frame, the Sun is playful and communicative. This is the time of information exchange, sharing, exploring.

The sign of Gemini or the third house in the chart is all about the joy of belonging to a group, sharing, showing, marketing. The ruler of this sign is the planet Mercury, which is here diurnal (through daytime) according to Ptolemy's Table of Essential Dignities. This is also the male sign, the element is the air and the colors are yellow, orange and all pastel shades. Gemini is the mutable sign and planet Mercury rules Wednesday. Countries under this sign are Belgium, Iceland, Kuwait, Tunisia.

Organs under Mercury's or Gemini's government are hands, lungs, and brain (together with Jupiter). He is all about neurology, transport of information through the body, its logistics. These are the processes where the sign of Gemini is beyond being just shallow because it shows our capacity to breathe and to distribute the nutritious matter through the whole body.

Natives born under the sign of Twins in most cases have a sibling and very close relationship with them. Besides this fact, they are always surrounded by numerous friends and although those friendships are very changeable in nature, natives continue to grow the enormous circle of acquaintances. It's very important to know the proper person for a proper issue; this is the leading motive for any Gemini.

Their marriages or relationships are mostly far from being committed at least in their younger years. Later on, when other planets become dominant factors in their chart they can become faithful, but before this happens they have to live and relive the experiences of feeling joyous with multiple people. The usual case is two marriages, one which happened too early and was driven by passion and ruined by impatience, and the second one which happened when native started to feel old and realized that everyone around is in a committed relationship.

One unusual, but very common thing going on for young Twins is the fact that most of them have to go through very serious illnesses as babies and those health problems are frequently related to lungs or breathing in general. There is always some sort of drama going on in children's hospitals and after the hardest first year of life, everything that follows looks much better. Young Twins are very cheerful children, so joyous that you'll get often headaches just looking at them. They enjoy elementary school and all childish games and they want to stay in this protected land of childhood forever.

Just don't force them to learn about complicated sciences and thing of the past, because it will be extremely difficult for them to understand and totally useless for their careers. Good profession for Gemini natives is a journalist, marketer, teacher, instructor, reporter, editor, writer, seller, trader, lawyer. Others might complain that these are not so grandiose professions like being an architect or chemist, but without these professions, our world would stop. Someone needs to be the messenger between people and gods after all.

The Sun in Gemini or in the third house of the horoscope is all about the speech, imagination, skills, expertize, but regarding down to earth knowledge which is applicable in every day's life. This is also the game, the art of trading, exchanging any sort of information or assets, practicality, and intellectualism. Established in the sign of Aries and secured by Taurus, the Sun is now like a little child ready to explore the neighborhood. Everything is new and exciting and worth researching.

The Moon in Gemini or placed in the third house describes the restless soul and spirit. I want to be here and there, in the best case scenario, at the same time and I love to hear about this and that, mostly nothing important, but it doesn't matter. People with the Moon positioned like this love to drive around the city, frequent short travels and fast food places, especially the street sold foods. Their relationship with their mother looks like a teenager friendship and communication is flowing free, but mostly about non-essential issues.

Mercury in Gemini or in the third area of the chart is in his own place. This is the image of an investigative journalist, speculative trader, entrepreneur, marketer, someone who works with children, like teachers in elementary schools and kindergartens. It's all about the play of life, all about bubbling and chatting and building something new seamlessly out of nothing, i.e., magazines, newspapers, websites, nothing too deep. When positioned negatively, this Mercury indicates mental problems, Autism Spectrum Disorder or ASD, even bipolar behavior.

Venus in Gemini is the image of a girl or a boy, or whatever you like her or him to be. Also Venus and Mercury in close or tense aspects with Uranus can indicate a homosexual or bisexual person too. But more important for this Venus is her girly or boyish appearance. Her body is not developed fully like in a grown woman, her legs are long and thin and she is the moment of glory for the fashion industry because every piece of clothing on her looks exactly like when it's on the hanger. She is about parties and gossiping, about shopping and spending her time in cafes and in the city.

Mars in Gemini or placed in the third house is the evident sign for the entrepreneurial spirit. From every penny, he will make two, from any garbage information he will make pure gold. He will raise his empire on marketing, selling fog, selling some shallow educational stuff applicable in business. He will use his power in the world of communication and when involved in construction building he will focus on the downtowns of big cities – small and practical apartments, but in the heart of the world.

This Mars is also exceptionally good when it comes to martial arts instructors, someone who has to teach, explain and fight at the same time. These are strong fists too. And if positioned negatively, this is the small street criminal, punches or slaps.

Jupiter placed in the sign of Gemini is in his sign of detriment; the same applies for the third house in personal horoscopes. This planet doesn't feel good here, because the deep and broad knowledge it carries can't be expressed completely through the certain shallowness of celestial Twins. In good aspects, this indicates someone who is very talented in sports, especially group sports like basketball and some natives seems to grow very tall with this position. Negatively speaking this can lead to some cognitive problems, ASD again, because fats and neurology are not composed properly in the brain tissue.

Saturn in Gemini points to some verbal problems; the person seems too slow, not capable of verbalizing or expressing thoughts fast enough. This also indicates some misunderstandings with siblings, especially younger ones, troubles with lungs and neurology. This is good for building business in the later part of life, though.

Uranus in Gemini or placed in the third area of the chart is about disruptions of the speech or the ideas. Often bipolar, ASD which can be used in the world of new communication technologies, odd ideas, new solutions, out of the box type of thinking if other aspects are confirming the strength of Uranus. This is good for electricians, online speakers, TV reporters. It also indicates some sudden events in the life of native which will take place in the neighborhood or nearby, when other transits trigger this planetary placement.

Neptune in Gemini is the symbol for a great writer or a liar depending on other aspects, but it's usually both. Something odd can happen in the neighborhood, a person gets inspired while walking or talking with neighbors. Strange events inspire this person, they are mindful of mythical inspiration, this is great for poets and science fiction novelists. At the same time, a person with Neptune in the third house will always find a church or any religious temple near his/her home and he/she will go there frequently no matter what is his/her religious background may be.

Pluto in Gemini is cunning, sly, witty, and tricky above everything else. This is the omen for the magnificent manipulator, someone who does horrible things in a childish manner. They have unusual intelligence, but it is always accompanied with sarcasm.

CANCER

The Sun transits through the sign of Cancer from the 21st of June until the 22nd of July and during this period of time, the Sun is about nurturing, home and motherly figures. This is the symbol for taking care, being intuitive and sensitive.

The sign of Cancer or the fourth house has the main theme of inner protection, safety provided by family and ancestral origin. The ruler of this sign is the Moon, which is here both diurnal and nocturnal according to Ptolemy's Table of Essential Dignities. This is also the female sign, the element is the water and the colors are blue, silver and all pearly shades. Cancer is the cardinal sign and the Moon rules during Monday. Countries under this sign are USA, Holland, Madagascar, and Bahamas.

Organs under the Moon's or Cancer's rulership are stomach, breasts, and womb, but in the case when the baby is inside the mother. This is also the symbol for the egg in a woman or any animal. This is the flow of water inside of us and therefore, it's imperative for females. Any organ filled with water becomes the Moon's belonging in those moments of fullness.

This is the symbol for big, watery eyes, commonly blue, babies and nutrition. Any pregnant woman is under the rulership of the Moon. Moodiness is a frequent flow of emotions, extreme sensitivity, night time, lakes, greater water surface with the full Moon mirroring in it, mirrors, tears, pearls. Constant changes in incomes, schedules, feelings. Good for dairy production, taking care of children, babies, nursing, taking care of elderly people, running restaurants, hotels, hostels.

The Sun in Cancer or placed in the fourth house of the chart describes sensitive person attached to mother, family or ancestors in general. Patriotism is strong here, although the Sun doesn't show his powers openly. This represents the nation, national pride, and heritage. Everything which deals with ideas of helping others through genuine care will be shown through this Sun. Perhaps it's too soft, but this Sun is not weak in the sign of Crab, it just doesn't want to show off and parade as it does in other signs. Their place of residence looks humble from the outside, but marvelous inside.

This Moon in Cancer is in its own house. This Moon feels protected and there is a clear lineage of women ancestors from whom the native learns about life, care, and support. This is the symbol of fertility, but at the same time, it indicates the frequent moves of the entire family. The kitchen is the prominent place for family gathering and many meals are based on milk, cheese and especially butter. The native with this placement knows how to heal members of the family, specifically children, with warm milk with spices and honey, soups, and teas. Although attached to the home, this native will often move to new locations and he will tend to settle down beside a lake or a larger pond.

Mercury placed in this sign of the fourth house indicates that person is very attached to the home, gains "down to earth" every day's knowledge usually from the mother, many people are transiting through the home, neighbors, friends, house full of siblings. There is a lot of information exchanged through mother or home environment, good for people who are working remotely online. They want small apartments, but close to the center of cities, small kitchens, small chairs or rooms, small items.

Venus in Cancer or placed in the fourth house of horoscope usually portraits the woman with big eyes, round face, bigger breasts, prone to weight gains due to excess water in her body. She is sensitive, focused on family, nurturing, somewhat conservative. Loves romance, nice items, nice manners. This is the symbol for the hidden mother in any woman, a lot of female friends, love can be found in the home through a visitor. She values security above all and she will be faithful in any sense of the word, to any man who is protecting her. Her complete soul will belong to her family.

Mars in Cancer or specially placed in the fourth house is in its fall here. Generally speaking, this is the worst position for the warrior. Just imagine the situation of letting the soldier take care of a baby, or letting a heavily armed warrior in the kitchen. His nature is fiery and he will cause all sorts of disputes in the home. In personal relationships, this is the image of a couple in a constant fight, verbal or physical. The man can abuse his wife, but at the same time, his whole family. The same goes for an aggressive woman. Fiery weapons held in the home, the danger of shooting, the danger of something burning in the kitchen, constant danger of fires. In the best case scenario, this is the person who constantly does some repairs or improvements in the home, so the drilling and breaking of the walls are a never-ending annoying sound for the entire family. And because Mars is so weak here, the native can become the bravest one, because he/she had to learn how to fight with everyone from the earliest age. Hot foods, stomachache, and a metabolism so fast that it tends to burn out the body earlier in life.

Jupiter in Cancer and divinely placed in the fourth house is in the sign of its exaltation. It's the common belief that this Jupiter can bring the expansion of the family's properties and wealth in general, but the truth is somewhat different than just this one aspect. This is the sign of exaltation for the big celestial guru, because higher knowledge should be inherited from the mother and female lineage in the family. From an early age, the mother should be the one to teach her children about fine manners, ability to listen and to feel, to absorb positive information, good foods, and stable emotions. This is the excellent position to feel protected from the inside, because Mars and the Sun are in charge of the outer protection, fighting and winning in the male style. Jupiter placed here is all about refined education and the healthy educational and intellectual abilities derived from healthy food and having a healthy mother. This is also the sign that properties are huge, food is plentiful and the surrounding area of the home is reflecting nature, meaning that there are lots of parks there, areas for sporting activities and even a temple related to the religion of origin.

Saturn in Cancer is in the sign of his detriment, unfortunately. This indicates obstacles in relation to the mother, chronic diseases, usually derived from sensitive stomach, problems with digestion, allergies to dairy, allergies to everything which came from the female lineage. Problems with heating, a person is often cold and catches colds in the house, the cold and dry atmosphere among the members of the family, growing up with grandparents and in many cases, the grandmother takes the role of the mother. This is a good position for producing ice-creams, distilled drinks, creating an exclusive retreat out of the old property, vineries, houses made of stones.

Uranus in Cancer announces frequent changes regarding home, moving in a sudden manner, a lot of uncertainty, neurotic mother, problems with electricity, irregular digestion, irregular childhood, growing amongst "crazy" or at least unusual people, growing beside electricity plant, problems with electricity, electrical devices behave out of control, especially in the kitchen, someone experiments with all sorts of technical items in the home, inventors, disruptors.

Neptune in the sign of Crab or placed in the fourth house of the chart indicates very foggy problems at home. The mother could have some eyesight issues; there could be an alcoholic always present, if not at home, then one of the close neighbors is prone to addiction of some sort, words and emotions are not clear, floods coming from the bathroom, spilled milk, always something boiling with the danger of exploding. Someone practicing homeopathy or creating pharmaceutical drugs from home. Home factory of illegal drugs, tarot card readers, something chemical or alchemical always going on. Frequent problems with bacterial infection and food poisoning. Some good advice is to avoid mushrooms.

Pluto in Cancer or placed in the fourth house indicates that some sort of the criminal act was done regarding ancestors. There could be a body buried underneath the home or around the property. A sudden explosion, crime, murder. On the positive side of this aspect, the native can discover a hidden treasure or any sort hiding in his home or origin.

LEO

The Sun transits through the sign of Leo from the 22nd of July until the 23rd of August and during this period of time the Sun is about dignity, pride, and domination. This is the symbol for royalty, entertainment, and children.

The sign of Leo or the fifth house is all about ruling over others, being just and doing well. The ruler of this sign is the Sun, which is here both diurnal and nocturnal according to Ptolemy's Table of Essential Dignities. This is the male sign, the element is the fire and the colors are yellow, gold and all glittery shades. Leo is the fixed sign and the Sun rules during Sunday. Countries under this sign are France, Italy, Mongolia, Bolivia.

Organs under the Sun's or Leo's rulership are the heart, spine and bone marrow. This is also the symbol of the life itself because the Sun is the light or the fire within. Natives born in this sign almost never get cancer of any kind and they manage to eliminate diseases very fast. However, they are in the greater danger of having a heart attack.

Odd but true, Leo has two sides of his character. He is like a child, enthusiastic about everything, open-minded and always in a good mood – he shines like the Sun. On the other side, he is the great organizer, structured and orderly leader with the clear set of intentions and instructions. He loves tradition and national history, he exalts in luxury, but only when he is the one, the alpha. He is the big hearted and large-minded individual with the established sense of hierarchy.

This native resolves all disputes in gentleman's manner, there is no point for jealousy because he/she is the best one and if the love partner is not clear or doesn't understand this, native will just leave with pride to find someone else who will respect him/her more. Marriage usually happens in the middle age when he had already accomplished something grand in his own life and this marriage is usually with the "trophy partner".

Children of the Lion are courageous and they should spend their times together with others learning to treat everyone equally. With afflicted planets, these children tend to gain weight very early in life.

The Sun in Leo or placed in the fifth house of horoscope is the basic image of the king (or queen), good heritage, dignity, and honesty. This is the person with strong principles and ordered mind, someone who loves formalism, good manners and open and honest conversation. In the negative context, this can also point toward snobbism, vanity or arrogance. This person has bright, often light eyes, greyish, wide forehead, curly hair, and strong stature. Later in life, the native is prone to become stubby. She has a talent for acting, drama, entertainment, and humor in general. Childish, but with the pure heart and this is the image of a child wanting to rule the whole world. Coat of arms, lions, flags, parades, bees, baroque – they all belong to Leo and the mighty Sun.

The Moon in Leo or placed in the fifth house can be a bit dried out when it comes to emotions. Feelings are present, but they are covered with a sense of duty and common sense. The native feels great love toward children and enjoys the idea to have many of them, but this is also the sign of having just one child in most cases. However, this is the wonderful placement for entertainment industry or working as the teacher in elementary school. There is increased flow through the heart, but a mobile spine at the same time.

Mercury in the sign of Leo or placed in the fifth area of the chart is the gift of a great speaker, especially when it comes to motivation. This Mercury is capable to mobilize masses from their depressive state of mind into any adventures, to make them go to war, build the fortress or calm down. These are also all expensive vehicles and the children of the rich people, who are capable of expanding the industries of their parents or just to enjoy their fortune and without fail to record experiences of a luxury life through social media.

Venus in the sign of Leo is always dressed to impress. She is branded from head to toe, and even if she doesn't possess means to wear expensive items yet, she will find some appropriate clothes which will resemble her dream to be dominant. This is the symbol for gold, exquisite jewelry, high heeled shoes with red soles, and small handbags with golden or platinum credit cards inside. Usually, her hair is long and blond, and she tries to keep her body in the best shape as long as she can. A native with this position of Venus finds love in the places of celebration, theaters or receptions. This is someone who will appear just in quality or luxury places and search for the adequate partner. Reason is leading the feelings and even when the third party gets involved, the native resolves the unpleasant situation without jealousy by just leaving in dignity.

Mars in Leo or in the fifth house indicates the soldier who wants to show off. This is the leader on the military parade. The pompous king who lives for adoration coming from his people. This is the portrait of a person who needs to be on the top and who will do anything to get there. At the same time, this indicates troubles with heart, easy exhaustion, passion and rage for life which can easily turn into weakness or illness. Good for practicing sports though.

Jupiter in Leo or placed in the fifth house is a person with a big heart in the positive and negative sense of the word. This could be the marvelous teacher, magnificent actor, someone who loves children and is blessed with very educated and successful progeny. At the same time, in the case that Jupiter receives negative aspects coming from other planets, this can be the person who wants to act like he/she is rich, educated and successful, but in reality, all those attempts fail with public humiliation. This can also be the lottery winners in some cases and problems with fat deposits in the arteries too.

Saturn in Leo is all about longing for progeny because this is the sign of his detriment. Usually, people with this position of Saturn want very passionately to become parents, but their wish comes true later in life and they always tend to have fewer children than they wished for. In bad aspects, this signifies afflictions with children, problematic romances, and a sad love life. Saturn here is also the sign of the great leader or politician, but someone who will have to rise through oppression or he will fall in shame. Changes in politics, turnarounds, turmoil, fall of the royal house.

Uranus in Leo creates special situations. This is someone who comes from the lower social rank and through the ideas of anarchy, communism or social politics tends to ruin the established system only to position him/herself as the next ruler. This is the image for crimes in high society, for exclusive frauds and disruptors of tradition. Placed in the fifth house,

Uranus indicates highly unstable love life, frequent relationships with psychologically immature partners and electrically disrupted heart.

Neptune in Leo is the clear sign of an unclear love life. Children might not belong to the native, they could be spurious, or the native could create children and then just disappear from their lives. This is the sign of love affairs; disrupted love life followed with all sorts of sexual disorders, love for illegal substances, especially in the liquid or gas states. This is also an indication of bacterial or viral infection of the heart or something unclear when it comes to heart or spinal function. On the positive side, these are talented musicians or poets.

Pluto placed in the fifth house or in the sign of Leo, if in the significant aspects with other celestial bodies, will create a sudden and great emperor in politics, in business, in entertainment. Everything around this person will be grandiose, destined and doomed. Also, this is the symbol for powerful children, exceptional life force coming straight from the heart, raw behavior, for avatars and gurus with supernatural powers, sudden death, unexplained murder.

VIRGO

The Sun transits through the sign of Virgo from the 23rd of August until the 23rd of September and during this period of time, the Sun is about collecting the fruits, healing, and serving. This is the symbol for the fullness of the autumn, hard workers, and natural healers.

The sign of Virgo or the sixth house is all about fixing, ordering or editing, being in service and doing the best for others. The ruler of this sign is the planet Mercury, which is here both nocturnal (during the night) according to a Ptolemy's Table of Essential Dignities. This is the female sign, the element is the earth and the colors are brown, golden brown, yellow, brown-red and all colors of the fall months. Virgo is the mutable sign and Mercury rules during Wednesday. Countries under this sign are Greece, Turkey, Brazil, Mexico, Switzerland.

Organs under Virgo's or Mercury's rulership are small intestine, spleen, and pancreas. This is also the symbol for the complete health of the body because Virgo controls our metabolic processes.

Virgo is known as the excellent worker, someone who serves others, a person with tremendous analytical abilities, sometimes neat picky, but with good intentions. They tend to become excellent doctors, lawyers, writers, administrative workers, thriving in all these professions, which are demanding precise and timely data.

Virgos will have stable marriages, but only after they go through a crisis of adjusting to their partner, and they, above all other signs, can be too demanding in the terms of clean, scheduled and precise living conditions. Little Virgo children should be involved with education, especially natural sciences because their minds will very quickly awake and they will take control over their future if directed properly from an early age.

The Sun in Virgo or placed in the sixth house of the horoscope demonstrates a darker type or person, someone slim and not very tall. This position of the Sun shows the natural ability for serving others or generally being of service toward anyone or anything in life. Great doctors are born in this sign, as well as nurses, natural healers, and nutritionists. This is also auspicious for administrative works, extended writing, editing or checking and rechecking. What has been sowed in the springtime, time of Aries and Taurus, now is reaped. This is the period of the year where we take the look back at the agricultural results and make necessary calculations for the future.

The Moon in the sign of Virgo or placed in the sixth area of the chart describes the person with the sensitive stomach, many minor illnesses, bloating, but this placement also indicates working with women, in the female environment or frequent contacts with many people. This is an excellent position for taking care of babies or elderly people. Women or a motherly figure in the native's life can also behave like a small enemy. This is someone who is a good psychologist or a social worker.

Mercury in the sign of the Virgin shows an excellent writer, editor, someone who will very thoroughly control and correct other people's papers or words. This is also someone who is magnificently talented for the healing of any sort, but especially natural methods. This person uses the wide knowledge regarding herbs, light exercises like yoga or qigong, homeopathy, nutrition and those methodologies the native had tried on him/herself first, because of the earlier digestive disputes. Food heals everything, a person might often claim, with the same passion and fire as one Leo claims that the Sun cures everything. On the negative side of the Virgin, this Mercury is prone to exhausting verbal fights, talks too much in general and annoys children or children are annoying to this native.

Venus in Virgo or positioned in the sixth house of the chart is the worst place for this essence of pleasure. Venus is in the sign of its fall here in the astrological sense. Too much analyzing, too much realism, work is hard and people are looking at the soil, crops and fruit trees, not noticing how beautiful this Venus is. She also grows in poverty here and she has to find a way out, trough calculations related to the perfect choice for marriage, or through using her beauty, body or clever mind to secure her future, but those details will mainly depend upon other planetary aspects too.

Mars placed in the sixth house of the sign of the Virgin is the clear sign of digestive or serious inflammatory problems with the gut. And diabetes belongs to this category. A person is usually allergic to grains and from the grains, all other health problems arise. But at this place, Mars also indicates the elevated levels of stress, working in the aggressive kind of environment, meeting many furious younger men and dealing with them. The native also has a very analytical type of reasoning and this person is really diligent. This is a great position for scientific or medical research, planning and designing machinery or real-estate blueprints.

Jupiter is in the sign of his detriment in the sign of Virgo or generally speaking, this great teacher feels badly placed in the sixth house which deals with daily obligations and usually non-important matters when the sea of knowledge is waiting to be found somewhere far. This is the avatar that is standing on the edge of the farmer's market trying to sell eggs or vegetables. He will surely have some hard times to finish this task because in that particular place people are less interested in his insights about the perfect cosmic shapes of the egg or the structure of energy inside one apple. Jupiter feels here very restricted and misunderstood. This position also indicates gaining fats around the waist area. This is good for using the scientific agricultural method on the large properties.

Saturn placed in the sign of the Virgin and especially in the sixth house describes annoying chronic diseases and this might be the punishment for the native for not becoming a doctor because greatest diagnostics are born with their Saturn in Virgo. This is the case when the mind goes very deep searching and finding the real cause of any disease. This can also be the indication for gallbladder stones or very slow and sensitive digestion. This Saturn points to the poor ancestors who probably had to cope with the hunger and oppression to survive. On the positive side, this is the extremely good position if the native is in the industry of dried foods, like dried fruits and vegetables. Good for storing and selling grains, nuts, and seeds, also for the "dry" foods like biscuits.

Uranus in Virgo or placed in the sixth house can describe the sudden problems with pancreas, diabetes, strange sensitivity of the gut caused by electricity or any form of EMF waves, causing danger with some modern types of diagnostics, like the ultrasound. On the positive side, this is the image of the excellent radiologist or, generally, a doctor who deals with latest diagnostic machinery. This is also the symbol for the sudden destruction of crops caused by lighting and storms, and very serious viral infections going on in the guts.

Neptune in the sign of Virgin is the archaic symbol for the holy smoke. This is the clear inclination toward smoking tobacco or any other herb, especially those with hallucinogenic traits. This is a very dangerous placement for people who are prone to food poisoning, extremely toxic mushrooms, and all chemicals used for food preservation or for the purposes of the modern agriculture. This is the sign of unclear bacterial infection of the guts and of the crops in the field too. On the positive side, this Neptune placed in the sixth house can give talent for imagination and excellent storytelling if supported by other planets.

Pluto placed in the sign of Virgo or positioned in the sixth house if in major aspects with the other important celestial bodies, can point in the direction of discovering hidden or, most likely, buried treasure on the family's property. This can also be the sign that the native can suddenly realize that some ancestral heritage can be used in marvelous ways, while on the negative side this is a tumor or a bullet in the stomach, horrible or magnificent health depending on other aspects.

LIBRA

The Sun transits through the sign of Libra from the 23rd of September until the 23rd of October and during this period of time, the Sun is about relationships, justice, and balance. This is the symbol for the business or marital partnerships, always focused on harmony.

The sign of Libra or the seventh house is all about dealing with others, being just, accomplishing the balance and success of both or all parties. The ruler of this sign is the planet Venus, which is here diurnal (during the day) according to a Ptolemy's Table of Essential Dignities. This is the male sign, the element is the air and the colors are green, light blue, turquoise, all gentle colors. Libra is the cardinal sign and Venus rules during Friday. Countries under this sign are Austria, Argentina, Tibet, Canada, Saudi Arabia.

Organs under Libra's or Venus's rulership are: kidneys and they are in the direct relations with the head (sign of Aries) in regards to controlling the blood pressure. This is also the symbolic sign describing how we function in the outer world receiving and answering to outer conditions.

Libra is the most famous sign of the beauty ideals, harmony between people and ideas of justice. However, on the negative side, this sign is full of snobbism, shallow behavior and pretending. Natives can be nice on the surface, but deep down in their souls, they are full of insecurities and therefore need established sets of rules. Generally, Librans are afraid of loneliness and when desperate they will commit to anyone willing to be with them. If the marriage starts earlier in life, it will usually break, but the later or the second marriage will last forever. Children of this sign should be thought to be independent and with a strong will, capable of making and sticking to their own decisions.

The Sun in the sign of Libra is in its fall. In other words, this in the worst possible place for the Sun. This means that the will of the person is weak because it is directed toward others. In this time of the year, everything is preparing to die or to sleep, harvest season is ending, and the whole nature is calming down. In ancient religions, this time was considered as the true beginning of the year because "And there was evening and there was morning, the first day" Bible, Book of Genesis, 1:3-5, everything begins from the dark, even before its conception, while being just the idea. Doing for others and having in mind their needs first is the death of the ego, therefore death for the Sun.

The Moon in the sign of Libra or in the seventh house is not such a good position either. Not so bad, like this is the case with the Sun, but still not very useful because the mind of the person is driven by emotions and those emotions are often scattered all around trying to be everywhere in every moment being present for everyone. This is hardly possible and many of the natives with this position of the Moon are considered to be shallow in their emotions. On the other side, this is the image of someone who lives for and through the social admiration. All of those fantasy or fake lives shown on social media platforms are the mirror reflection of this Libra's Moon. Positively speaking, a person needs to be close to someone through committed love or a business partner to be able to feel full and useful. In some cases, this is the indication of volatility in marriage or multiple marriages in the life of this person.

Mercury in the seventh house or in the sign of Scales is the clear image of the great lawyer, public speaker, someone who loves to show his words, speech or ideas in public. This is also the indication for the talented actor capable of memorizing huge amounts of dialogs. Excellent entrepreneur, even better negotiator. On the negative side, this person can be tricky and if Mercury receives negative aspects, this will show grandeur liar or deceiver. In any case, the native's children will be well raised and with good manners.

Venus in the sign of Libra or positioned in the seventh house is in its own home. However, this Venus is focused on relationships, instead of just material possessions. These possessions, in fact, in the kingdom of Libra are in the realm of spiritual, being airy in nature. These are all about beauty, balance, harmony, proper measure, proper manners, and the ability for lovely social communication. Great for partnerships of any kind. This Venus has slim, fairy body, lighter eyes or hair with delicate and beautiful moves, which are not so erotic in their nature, but more prone to elegancy.

Mars in the sign of Libra or positioned in the seventh house is in his sign of detriment. This Mars doesn't feel so good in the circle of women, in the ceremonial type of situations or mannered conversation. Especially in the seventh house, it can indicate frequent marital disputes and even a divorce. A person usually knows what is right and what is wrong in the relationship, but their partner simply can't adjust to harmonious life together and this is the source of all troubles. On the positive side, this is one very strategically oriented Mars. Ancient martial arts are based on this position due to the fact that they all have a foundation in the idea of harmony. The game of chess also belongs to this category.

Jupiter in the sign of Libra or placed in the seventh house of the chart describes the person who has good abilities when it comes to aesthetics, someone who is loved and respected in society and, most likely, someone who is very popular and can easily spread ideas in certain social circles. This is also the respected actor or performer of any kind of art. The person with this position tends to rise in society after marriage, but it can be good for business partnerships too. If afflicted this planet gives some sort of religious disputes with the spouse or even troubles in society regarding personal religious or spiritual views.

Saturn in the sign of Scales exalts in that particular place, and this is also the case when it's in the seventh house. A person might wait a bit longer to get married, but once this marriage happens, it will be unbreakable. Saturn is all about duty and justice, and in the sign of Libra, this planet can show all of his power amongst other people surrounding the native with this position. It's pretty easy to be the best one and stand alone on the top of the mountain of success, which is the case with Saturn in Capricorn. However, it's far more demanding to be fair, focused and balanced when the baby is crying, the husband needs his dinner, while your mother is on the phone asking did you call her dentist, for instance. This is the excellent example of being in balance and with the stable mind when everything around you is crashing down. This is the real and the most powerful emanation of the planet Saturn. In relation to this is the story about the piece of coal, which had to go through extreme temperatures and pressures to become the diamond.

Uranus in Libra or placed in the seventh house is always about the partnership disruptions, divorces or marrying divorced person. These are fast and unstable partnerships, even in the business sense.

Neptune in Libra or especially when this planet is positioned in the seventh house indicates something unclear regarding marriage. In the best case scenario, a person will marry someone with eye problems or someone involved in film or TV acting. In all other cases, this could be the sign of lying or cheating in marriage and in business.

Pluto in the sign of Libra or when it's forming significant aspects with the other planets from the seventh house tends to behave in the brutal sense to the public. If the aspects Pluto makes are negative, this is someone who is hated by everyone, and popular due to this fact. It can also be related to a fated love stories or complete withdrawal from others.

SCORPIO

The Sun transits through the sign of Libra from the 23rd of October until the 22nd of November and during this period of time the Sun is about death, depths, and resurrection. This is the symbol for the transformation, sexual energy, as well as unearned incomes.

The sign of Scorpio or the eighth house is all about transforming the ideas, body, diving deep into the world of the occult or unknown. The ruler of this sign is the planet Mars, which is here nocturnal (during the night) according to Ptolemy's Table of Essential Dignities. This is the female sign, the element is the water and the colors are black, of course, burgundy red and purple. Scorpio is the fixed sign and Mars rules during Tuesday. After its discovery, planet Pluto is generally considered to be the co-ruler of this sign together with Mars. Countries under this sign are Turkey, Panama, Lebanon, Cambodia, Angola.

Organs under Scorpio's rulership are: the genitals and all excretion organs. This is also the symbolic sign describing how the life is transformed in us through the energy of passion, creating a new being, and also what we need to let go of to become free.

This is the sign of the "other side". The person had to go through some harsh experience in life, perhaps even more of those experiences to become initiated into the real Scorpion. This is the special sign because its transformations are always going through three phases. First, the native is a Scorpio, low, furious and bad. Then it becomes the Eagle, above everyone else, but vengeful. And the third stage is when the native becomes the Phoenix or the Dragon, which depends on the astrological tradition of a certain area. In this phase, a person is higher than anyone else, but it can also transform lives and this time in a powerful and positive way.

The Sun in the sign of Scorpio or placed in the eighth house of the chart is all about very dramatic transformations throughout the whole life. This Sun already died in the sign of Libra, so now it's wandering through the underworld seeking for the purpose and the meaning, not just of life, but of death itself. The will is here focused, magnetic, dramatic and it searches for the way to make a breakthrough. This

Sun doesn't fear responsibility or risk, it can't and it won't stop in its pursuits, no matter whether the native with this position of the Sun achieves something or just watches.

The Moon in the sign of Scorpio or in the eighth house is in the sign of its fall, the worst place for sensitive Moon, indeed. The soul is forced to dive deep into the unknown and usually, the native with this position is forced to go through some serious problems from an early age. This person was hurt in a very horrible way due to disputes with the mother or any motherly figure around. He/she was emotionally abandoned and ridiculed by the ones this person needed the most, or in some cases, the mother couldn't protect the child because she had to go through tremendous pain. The second phase this Moon has to go through is self-hatred and hatred toward members of the family, tribe or anyone involved with a challenging experience. The Moon like this is capable of thinking and conducting any type of revenge and even black magic rituals. And the third step toward transformation is forgiveness. This Moon understands and forgives for all the troubles it had to experience and in those moments, it gains supernatural powers to heal others. This is a great placement for energy healers, exquisite doctors, pharmacists or chemists.

Mercury positioned in the eighth house or in the sign of Scorpio is the clear indication for someone who is talented in occult sciences or with the gift of clairvoyance. This is great for astrologers, tarot card readers and similar professions. At the same time, this is the excellent position for diagnostics in medicine, but the native might have a dirty or simply rude way of speaking.

Venus in the sign of Scorpio or placed in the eighth house is in its sign of detriment. The queen of pleasure is lost in the darkness and here she has nowhere to turn but directly to the king of the underworld. She is prone to sexuality, her beauty can become cheap or aggressive depending on the other planetary positions and she thrives through challenging or lost romances. The person with this position of the planet Venus had his/her heart broken many times and love can even be found through some very tragic events. Although mainly considered as cheap, this Venus can be an exclusive type of a woman who went through all sorts of dramatic events in her life and now became excellent in the skills of war and strategic thinking. She is the type of a perfect female warrior which is used in the battle when all other options have failed. And consequently, she is the queen in the game of chess who will be sacrificed for victory. A woman with this mission is the highest symbol for this Venus.

Mars in Scorpio is in his own kingdom, but with some slight differences than in his other house – Aries. Here this planet is in his night mode, so we no longer deal with that naïve and open-minded type of Mars. This planet in Scorpio is known as the excellent strategist, he is something like the war advisor for the Sun and his opinion, targets, and goals are always hidden. Mars is the warrior who is skilled and extremely precise with weapons, but unlike the Aries Mars who loves to join forces with others, this one thrives when he works alone. This is the image of the hitman, the sniper or someone who waits in the dark corner of the street with a knife. In the medical sense, this is the perfect position for the best surgeons, but if this is not the case, then the native falls ill in a sudden manner and most of those illnesses are acute, hard, but short lasting. These are commonly inflammations of the sexual organs or bladder.

Jupiter placed in Scorpio or in the eighth house of the chart can lead a person toward such extensive and positive transformations that this person can become much more skilled, better or far in front of everyone else in life. If negatively aspected, in this case, Jupiter will direct such a person toward a leading position, but in a shameful business, like running a mafia or dangerous religious cult. This position also indicates great returns on investments or a marriage with a person who makes a significant income.

Saturn placed in the eighth house of the horoscope or in the sign of Scorpio describes a long life, but usually with long chronic illnesses too. The person might have problems with kidney stones or sand and something is always wrong with the sexual drive or large intestine. On the positive side, this is good for investing in precious metals and stones, and also properties, especially old and valuable ones.

Uranus in Scorpio or in the eighth house can be very dangerous because Uranus is considered to be the higher octave of the planet Mercury. This Uranus can indicate sexual perversion, harsh character or sudden death caused by electricity. The energy created in this area of the chart is too strong, and it causes disruptions and eruptions.

Neptune in the sign of Scorpio or placed in the eighth house points to the danger of drowning. Besides this, a person is in the constant danger of infection through water, bathing or sexual contacts. This is also a love of drugs, legal or illegal and if other aspects are supportive in a negative or positive way, this person can become a drug dealer or a pharmacist

Pluto placed in Scorpio or in the eighth house can be very peaceful if it's not in aspect with the other planets or triggered by their transits. If this Pluto is active in the chart, then this can be the sign of a great healer, but it can also point to the direction of a murderer, deadly explosions, fires, military graveyards and all things related to the symbolism of joined Mars and Pluto, which means fear, terror, and trauma.

SAGITTARIUS

The Sun transits through the sign of Sagittarius from the 22nd of November until the 21st of December and during this period of time the Sun is about discoveries, higher learning, and expansion. This is the symbol of the spirituality, joy of newness trough intellectual and physical activity.

The sign of Sagittarius or the ninth house is all about reaching for the higher ground and exploring the depthless quality of the human or a godly soul. The ruler of this sign is the planet Jupiter, which is here diurnal (during the day) according to Ptolemy's Table of Essential Dignities. This is the male sign, the element is fire and the colors are golden yellow and saffron orange. Sagittarius is the mutable sign and Jupiter rules during Thursday. Countries under this sign are Australia, Spain, China, South Africa, Kenya.

Organs under Sagittarius' rulership are the liver, buttocks, and thighs. This is also the symbolic sign describing how freedom is achieved after the drama coming from Scorpio, where we keep out the inner fire and how to reach it.

The sign of the Archer values his freedom the most and therefore earlier marriages usually end through divorce. Second marriage might be with the person with the greater age or cultural difference when most of the Sagittarians search for novelty and liberty is already satisfied. Children of this sign should be thought to respect social norms, but to spend most of their time outside pursuing sports and pieces of evidence in the field of natural sciences. The broadness of the mind or the human soul are their highest aims, so don't limit them and they will show their best.

Sun in the sign of Sagittarius or placed in the ninth house of the horoscope clearly describes the person who is prone to becoming a great teacher, the real guru for younger generations. This is also someone who loves to travel to distant places and delights through the ideas of constant growth and research. A person like this is always talented for comedy and even in the midst of very hard or demanding events, this person finds the way to lighten everyone around them. Physically this is the portrait of someone with a big or at least tall body, but if afflicted this Sun will show someone who is short and fat.

The Moon in the sign of Sagittarius or positioned in the ninth house is someone who is restless when it comes to traveling. This person will change many places and his home will be on the road. Later on in life, the native can settle through marriage, but most likely with the person who originates from completely different religious or cultural background. On this place, the soul is seeking for better answers than the ones which were given just through the official process of education. The mother figure is prominent in the native's life as someone who is truly educated, but at the same time bighearted and open-minded.

Mercury in the sign of Sagittarius is not in its best position because this is the sign of its detriment. And the same applies for the Mercury in the ninth house. The mind of the person is down to earth here where it's supposed to fly higher. It's like someone let the supermarket cashier into the university laboratory to supervise experiments, or it can look like the gathering of the traders in the temple. The person with this position lacks a deeper understanding of life and therefore shows as inadequate for the situations he/she has to go through. On the positive side, this is the image of the person who works on the supportive and administrative types of jobs for universities or spiritual organizations.

Venus placed in the sign of Sagittarius or placed in the ninth house of the horoscope is an indication that this person, or a woman, or a female energy in a native, will just love to travel to exotic destinations. A woman like this doesn't seek luxury and comfort; she delights in oriental scents, customs, and patterns. Her clothes can be sloppy, but colorful and she just loves the hippy style. Her desires are broad and related to erotica, not so much real passion. And she will never forget to show her long legs or talk about her Ph.D. Giving her the freedom to speak her mind and to move wherever she wants will be the best way to attach her to yourself.

Mars positioned in the ninth house or in the sign of Sagittarius is known for his good mood in any situation. This is truly strong, but at the same time, this is a peaceful Mars which uses his strength for some higher purposes than just fighting. These are the people who love horse riding, hunting, tennis, car races, tennis, archery, all those sports or activities which will move the person further, but at the same time indicate the certain dose of nobility. This type of Mars won't get provoked so easily, he will rather think about the whole situation with humor and probably decide to walk away from an excessive situation. This is the great position for archaeologists, travel guides, sports instructors and also doing business related to spiritual or religious themes or working with foreigners.

Jupiter in the sign of Sagittarius or placed in the ninth house can ensure magnificent success in philosophy and any natural sciences. This is someone who is generous, righteous and good-hearted, but at the same time, this is a person who is internally free and besides this, also has significant social and financial successes. This success is ensured in his plans, speculations or any type of endeavor too. Good positions for this native are a lawyer, judge, priest, organizer of others, but mostly in the field of spirituality. In good aspects, this person is noble with high moral standards and influence on others, while with affected Jupiter, this shows like someone who exaggerates in everything and this can lead him to failure in life and completely ruin his reputation.

Saturn in the sign of Sagittarius or placed in the ninth house of the chart is the portrait of a serious deep thinker and someone successful regarding metaphysical issues. This can also be an indicator for a great astronomer if other aspects are supporting. In usual cases, this is the sign of someone who wants to pursue higher education in the form of the university diploma, but due to circumstances the person can't achieve this, mainly due to the necessity of daily working tasks needed for financial survival. This is also the symbol for refugees, walls, obstacles trying to reach better living conditions, problems with authorities and issues with legal matters.

Uranus placed in the ninth house or in the sign of Sagittarius can pull the person toward spiritual disruptions in some sense. A person usually seeks to run away from national or family religious traditions and in this search finds many new teachings which are not appropriate or leave this person disappointed. If positioned well through aspects with other celestial bodies in the chart, this is the portrait of someone who is talented for incorporating the latest technology into traditional ways of learning, and also someone talented for astronomy, astrology and maintaining frequent contacts with technologically savvy foreign people.

Neptune in the sign of Sagittarius or positioned in the ninth house of the chart is someone who dreams about distant exotic places and those dreams are filled with fantasies of peace, meditation, rest, relaxing. In a good position, this person visits temples, especially monasteries where spiritual knowledge is delivered through wise and often foreign persons. In negative aspects, this is someone who can suffer from asthma, there is also the possibility of breathing problems related to hiking or alpinism, or generally speaking, problems with religious beliefs covered with illusions or inhaling illegal or harmful substances.

Pluto in the ninth house or placed in the sign of Archer is all about phantasm, ideological movements, and turnarounds which ruin cultural monuments, irrational philosophical systems planned for the future, using force to reach freedom, using pray to heal, complete transformation through religion.

CAPRICORN

The Sun transits through the sign of Capricorn from the 21st of December until the 20th of January and during this period of time the Sun is about hierarchy, structure, and power. This is the symbol for the established position, hard work, and dedication.

The sign of Capricorn or the tenth house is all about reaching the top of the mountain, corporate ladder, or any other type of reputation we project into the outer world. The ruler of this sign is the planet Saturn, which is here nocturnal (during the night) according to Ptolemy's Table of Essential Dignities. This is the female sign, the element is the earth and the colors are black, coal shades of gray and sometimes brown. Capricorn is the cardinal sign and Saturn rules during Saturday. Countries under this sign are Great Britain, India, Mexico, Sudan, Bulgaria.

Organs under Capricorn's rulership are bones in general, knees and teeth. This is also the symbolic sign describing how the position and reputation are fought for, established and maintained through constant hard work and focused efforts.

This is the sign of the strong family or national tradition. Through struggle, oppression and hard environmental conditions, the native will sharpen his/her skills and become very powerful, seeking for the better or the best of life. Capricorn is the sign of the true material wealth and people born like Goats will ensure their lives with the best lands, real-estates, and piles of gold. They tend to get married a little later in life, but those marriages are stable as rocks and their partners know what is expected of them right from the start. Children are shy and they should be encouraged to enjoy life more and to try to be more empathetic toward others.

The Sun in the sign of Capricorn or placed in the tenth house of the chart indicates the person who is goal oriented, has respectful and highly established fatherly figure in his/her life and seeks to repeat his father's success or usually do better. This person might feel lonely and isolated in the earlier ages, but in the second part of life, the native suddenly awakens, focuses and achieves success through dedication. The Sun doesn't feel particularly good in this sign; however, this Sun is absolutely certain that it can't get a position or gain possessions solely through the ego, but through using all sorts of interactions with others, positive as well as negative. Strong, but controlled and guided will is fully operational.

The Moon in the sign of Capricorn or placed in the tenth house is in the sign of its detriment. The Moon simply doesn't feel good in the cold and rough environment. Perhaps it can be good for a father's type of energy, but it surely doesn't suit the soul of the mother. This can be the indication that relationship with the mother was rather cold or she was unavailable for the native during the phase of childhood in some sense. Feelings are frozen or very slow in expression. This doesn't mean that this person is senseless in any way, but he/she is closed, conservative and afraid because the outer world is oppressive and even brutal.

Mercury in the sign of the Goat or placed in the tenth house points to someone who is slow, but meticulous during childhood years, probably with speech problems, and this person can even seem to be not so bright for people surrounding him/her. However, in the more mature phases of life, this Mercury starts to catch the general rules of life, especially business and becomes a very shrewd businessman. This is the great entrepreneurial spirit, someone capable of running multiple businesses at once.

Venus in the sign of Capricorn or placed in the tenth house is the portrait of a lady, simply put. In the second part of life, this Venus starts to show her beauty and magnificent sense of elegance. These are usually wives of powerful business and political figures, neatly dressed and with the excellent manners. When her hair becomes gray, she reaches the peak of her power. If she gets acquainted with the business or corporate world, then success can be found through female types of industries, like fashion, accessories, and cosmetics. Love is found through the area of work and in many cases, there is the age difference greater than seven years between marriage partners.

Mars in the sign of Capricorn or placed in the tenth house of the chart is a phenomenally good place for this Mars because this is the sign of his exaltation. This planet becomes the strongest here, not just in the terms of his physical power, but this is included also. He is at his peak because he has the focused mind and his will is made of steel. In most cases, he came from a very poor environment and he had to fight for everything in life. He is accustomed to hunger and to lacking the basic means in life. So, he fights and learns along his path. In the physical sense, this is one very naturally strong Mars because he didn't build his muscles spending time in the gym, but through physical work, which made him capable of wrestling with a bear, any bear in life. In the terms of a career, this position is great for real-estate business, construction building, and engineering, dealing with metallurgy or any highly developed industry.

Jupiter placed in the sign of Capricorn or in the tenth house of the horoscope is someone who achieved success in the public life, but through a long process or proving his/her skills or expertise. This process most likely came with the help of foreigners or priests and it seemed to everyone else that it was accomplished with the godly peace or in a noble manner. This is also the portrait of the supreme judge in the state, the highest priest or the best public speaker or a guru. The native can climb very high regarding careers, which are dealing with education, especially related to the business kinds of education.

However, Jupiter is in its fall here and he always feels limited by circumstances.

Saturn placed in his home sign, the sign of Capricorn or in the tenth house speaks volumes about the long and hard pursuit for security, expertise and recognition. This is someone who grew old trying to create his/her kingdom and now stands on the top of the world or on the top of the mountain. Saturn placed here is all about tradition, crypts, old castles with dungeons and dragons underneath. These are all servants, slaves and poor oppressed people. This is the sign of someone who loves to eat simple peasant food, goat's meat, burnt a bit, with dried foods also. If in positive aspects this is the indication for the rich and powerful person, not necessarily famous or loved by everyone. This is the symbol for properties, lands, wealth in the big sense of this world. Industries related to this position are mining, archeology, metallurgy, machinery and similar hard, but at the same time very profitable jobs.

Uranus in the sign of Capricorn or placed in the tenth house of the chart describes a very unusual career for the native. This can be the sign of someone who applies very advanced technologies and mixes them with traditional methods. Astronauts, IT engineers, inventors and many more fall into this category. In negative aspects, this is someone who changes careers frequently, doesn't get along with authorities and therefore pursues a unique type of career and recognition.

Neptune in the sign of the Goat or placed in the tenth house can indicate someone who is involved in the shady businesses or politics, but in very problematic ways which frequently include lies. If this planet is receiving positive aspects in the chart, then it indicates great success in the chemical, agro-chemical, pharmaceutical or oil industry and the person with this position can rise above everyone else if the planet Saturn is positioned well also.

Planet Pluto placed in the sign of Capricorn or in the tenth house can be the sign of the remarkable career in all areas which deal with engineering, machinery, real-estate, properties in general, excavations, mining and highest levels of banking. On the negative side, this is the aggressive oppression, military power, war criminal, dangerous magic and cults, production of weapons, dogs of wars, nuclear power plants and weapons.

AQUARIUS

The Sun transits through the sign of Aquarius from the 20th of January until the 18th of February and during this period of time, the Sun is about newness, equality, and diversity at the same time. This is the symbol for the technological and social advancement, as well as grouping of the people.

The sign of Aquarius or the eleventh house is all about being equal with others, uniting for the sake of the common cause and at the same time streaming for the higher ideal. The ruler of this sign is the planet Saturn, which is here diurnal (during the day) according to Ptolemy's Table of Essential Dignities. This is the male sign, the element is the air and the colors are light blue, silvery blue and washed out gray shades. Aquarius is the fixed sign and Saturn rules during Saturday. After its discovery, planet Uranus is considered to be the co-ruler together with Saturn. Countries under this sign are Russia, Iran, Syria, Sweden, Sri Lanka.

Organs under Aquarius' rulership are lower legs, complete neurology and lymphatic system. This is also the symbolic sign describing how our dreams can become the reality if we all unite, focus and work for mutual benefits.

Nothing is stable in this sign, especially marriages and relationships of any sort. People unite under one idea and then separate when conditions tend to change. Children are good hearted, but often without any manners and they should be thought to respect order a little bit more, and also they should be kept away from technological gadgets. But this is a lost battle in advance.

The Sun in the sign of Aquarius or placed in the eleventh house of the horoscope is its sign of fall here. This is the time of exhausting winter on the northern hemisphere and the Sun shows its face for a very short time during the day. At the same time, astrological interpretation points toward the sign of Leo where the Sun is in its home. Leo is the symbol for the ruler, the king, while Aquarius is the symbol for the people. And the Sun naturally doesn't feel supreme surrounded with those plain, raw and often rude souls. On the other side, the Sun placed here is all about the change and creating plans for the better future.

The Moon placed in the sign of Aquarius or in the eleventh area of the chart is describing someone who is prone to change and those emotional changes are highly dependent upon the changes going on the social circles of the native. A person with this position is interested and open toward anyone and any idea, but at the same time, the native lacks the deeper understanding how the life operates. Yes, it's not fair, the native often thinks and more often speaks, *why don't all rich people/corporations/countries just give up all money/properties/wealth to the poor and we will all be equal and happy*. At the same time, this person forgets about the hierarchy of power and the laws of evolution. There is not such a thing as being equal in this Universe and that is out of the reach or understanding of this Moon. On the positive side, it's easy to cheer up this person and the mother or the motherly figure was creative and joyous through this person's childhood.

Mercury placed in the sign of Aquarius or in the eleventh house could be, and in some rare cases is, the talent of the magnificent writer, if this person could manage to organize his/her mind and escape from shallow or daily disruptions. In all other cases, this is the real messenger and this person thrives in the careers related to IT technology, content writing, social media influence, journalism, trending and similar types of jobs which don't require deep understanding or proven and double checked information. If positioned negatively relative to other celestial bodies, this Mercury is capable to ruin its own reputation with rumors and gossips and hardly able to plan or to envision the future. The native just loves technological gadgets.

Venus placed in the eleventh house or in the sign of Aquarius is more about showing off in society than feeling the real pleasure inside. Love can be found in the places of mass gathering, like fairs, national celebrations, clubs, parties and of course, social media. In this particular horoscope house, love shouldn't be deep or dramatic; it's more about the leisure type and "look at me, look at us" representation. Erotica is present but without any real or lasting sexual passion. This Venus also thrives on sex exchanging games; she can be he, or even it, whatever that means in her/his/ its head. She loves to look different than the norm, but at the same time, she needs to be protected by the social circle which dresses or behaves in the same or similar manner.

Mars in the sign of Aquarius or placed in the eleventh house of the chart describes the person who is inclined generally in technology and engineering. These are all those guys who are prone to mechanical repairs related to cars, electricity, plumbing, construction building. This Mars is not the strongest and he is completely aware of this fact, but at the same time, he knows he can become unbeatable if he unites with others. If Mars receives negative aspects, then this can be the indication of a street gang membership, grouping for destruction causes. In positive aspects, this Mars unites with others to be able to make a breakthrough in technology, daily working tasks or exploring the unknown territories. Poor and oppressed groups of people who are seeking for their happiness elsewhere traveling long distances are the symbol for joined efforts of this type of masculine energy.

Jupiter in the sign of Aquarius or placed in the eleventh house is not in such perfect condition here, but this is far from being bad for the native's life. This person surrounds herself with a great number of other people and most of them are educated or at least influential in society. Networks of friends, business associates, valuable mentors, good social position, great plans for the future, these things are all covered and protected by the planet Jupiter in Aquarius. If in a positive aspect with Uranus, this can also indicate lottery winning or a sudden windfall of money. Also, Jupiter placed here can be the wonderful teacher for the masses and an excellent social worker. In negative aspects, the native has a distorted sense of spirituality and bad social position.

Saturn in the sign of Aquarius or placed in the eleventh house of horoscope is in his own house here, where this planet delights in the ideals of uniting the poor and turning against the established government or king or whoever is in charge. This is the symbol for washed out working uniforms, great movements of pioneers or refuges, hunger, but with the burning desire for a better future. At the same time, this points in the direction that person is surrounded with older or poor people, bounded by the same principles, beliefs, and prejudices.

Uranus in the sign of Aquarius or placed in the eleventh house of the horoscope speaks volumes about instability related to relationships or career. This is also someone who takes risky investments and in negative aspects, this is the person who is the blind follower of trends, easily changes his/her mind and the shallow thinker. In the positive aspects, this is the image of a great inventor, someone who stands out from all due to his/her unique way of thinking and living.

Neptune in the eleventh house or placed in the sign of Aquarius indicates someone who enjoys very foggy company. Something is not clear here when the friends are involved. They might be prone to illegal substances, actions or ideas. Good for electronic types of music or modern arts related to technology, bad for investments and planning.

Pluto in the eleventh house or placed in the sign of Aquarius, and if affected significantly by other planets, has the ability to turn friends into enemies.

This could also be the member or the leader of the very dangerous closed type of organization, or this can be someone with clairvoyant or visionary ideas.

PISCES

The Sun transits through the sign of Aquarius from the 18th of February until the 20th of March and during this period of time the Sun is about diving deep into the unknown cosmic sea, mysteries and hidden issues of creation. This is the symbol for spirituality, but in the personal and internal sense, isolation and seeking wisdom through silence.

The sign of Pisces or the twelfth house is all about being equal with the higher power, being alone in the sea of changes, diving into the self and at the same time diving into the divine. The ruler of this sign is the planet Jupiter, which is here nocturnal (during the night) according to Ptolemy's Table of Essential Dignities. This is the female sign, the element is the water and the colors are dark blue, silver, and all pearly shades. Pisces is the mutable sign and Jupiter rules during Thursday. After its discovery, planet Neptune is considered to be the co-ruler here together with Jupiter. Countries under this sign are Portugal, North Africa, Scandinavia, Namibia, Samoa.

Organs under Pisces' rulership are feet, blood, and complete circulatory system. This is also the symbolic sign describing our inner desires, fears, and readiness to explore the inner types of truths.

Pisceans are known as the best pharmacists, musicians, and spiritual leaders, although many of them can be perceived as confused and lost in this world. They usually tend to wait longer for the proper marital partner and the children born in this sign should be thought to be more social and realistic.

The Sun in the sign of Pisces or placed in the twelfth house of horoscope describes the person who is shy, patient and kind. This Sun doesn't use any of his entitled credits or special treatments. The native seems to have a very hard first third of life and finds success in reclusive types of professions. Basically, he seeks to help others and achieves this goal through the hospital or religious types of job, and often he can be seen as the lonely artist. In positive aspects, this native gets help or achieves success traveling and living overseas and in certain cases, he gets valuable help from highly educated foreigners.

The Moon in the sign of Pisces or placed in the twelfth house is the image of a person with very unclear feelings, lost in the sea of deep revelations and always changing. This person is highly sensitive, and there is something unusual in native's relationship with the mother. The mother could be absent, seriously ill or even dead if this position is negatively affected by other natal planets and person seeks to build his/her own ideal of motherly energy around this fact. The soul feels a deep loss and it always desires to come back home, wherever this spiritual and safe place is. If the mother is present, then she takes the role of a teacher, a real guru in the native's life and this education takes unusual forms, which can have extreme quality or be disastrous, depending on other aspects.

Mercury in the sign of Pisces or placed in the twelfth house is in his sign of fall and detriment here also. This planet is all about the transmission of information and especially verbal expression, and at this place, this can't be done. Words scatter, they lose their meaning and information is distorted. This is the place where a person shouldn't speak or write at all, where the mind and logic are drowned in the sea of wider knowledge than this Mercury will ever be able to understand. However, you can't prove this to the mercurial type of person. He/she will try in spite any advice to keep silent and make many mistakes along the way. This is also the sign of the danger of being robbed by a pickpocket, of being gossiped about and having some small, but very determined enemy.

Venus in the sign of Pisces or placed in the twelfth house of the horoscope is in her position of exaltation here. But don't get so excited too soon because this place is all about isolation and Venus can have the purest feelings and the best looks in Pisces and still stand alone. This is the greatest position for artistic pursuits, especially singing and poetry, not so good for marriage, because Venus is still in the sign which is the symbol of loneliness. She is lovely, romantic and delicate in her communication. Love can be found in all closed places, like hospitals, islands or distant foreign lands.

Mars in the sign of Pisces or in the twelfth house describes the introverted type of character. He is far from being weak in this weird place, but he is turned toward inner, deeper or higher breakthroughs, and he is simply not interested in the outer world. Good professions for this position are sailors, scientific researchers, all people who have to explore something away from the crowd and usual noise. If affected negatively, this native will have very powerful enemies, sudden and dangerous diseases and he could be even physically attacked in the dark. In positive aspects, this can be the military doctor or even a silent hero.

Jupiter placed in the sign of Pisces or in the twelfth house is in his own house here. This might mean some emotional or psychological instability, especially in the childhood, because native with this position simply feels that there is much more in life than just passing fancy and shining, but truly shallow objects, events or people. Later on, this person develops broader knowledge and starts to understand the magic of all realms of existence. This is a very auspicious position for people who aim for the highest types of university education, as well as people who are prone to become monks or priests. At the same time, this points in the direction of valuable help coming from the educated person or moving permanently very far, in most cases over the ocean. If affected, this Jupiter will describe a person who is lost in this world and ends up in the hospital or in the monastery.

Saturn in the sign of Fish or placed in the twelfth house is someone very emotionally close, prone to deep thinking and also prone to prolonged, chronic diseases. The person will surely have to deal with some hidden enemies and in most of the cases, those will be elderly and very powerful people. Many times this person will suffer from some serious trauma related to the people representing a religion of origin. If affected negatively by other aspects, this position could lead a native right to jail. In some cases, this might be working there as the guardian, manager or a doctor, but in extreme situations, this will mean imprisonment. Health is overall weak and the danger of blood clots is always present.

Uranus in the sign of Pisces or in the twelfth house portraits the person who delights around the ideas of how close is the end of the world, conspiracy theories and of course, extraterrestrial visitors. This is someone who is full of extraordinary and even fascinating ideas, but the real problem here is that this person lacks the focus or stable energy to make those ideas true. At the same time, this position can represent the danger of sudden and very challenging viral infections or attacks coming from a psychologically unstable person.

Neptune positioned in the twelfth house or in the sign of Pisces simply loves to reside here, because this is its home. Based on this place's inspiration, music, poetry or craziness can go sky high. In the sign of Aquarius Neptune loves pharmaceutical supplement, but here, this planet will go deep into natural types of healing, like herbalism or homeopathy. The person with this position feels the strong desire to run away from reality and in negative aspects, this could mean the danger of drowning or choking. Great for pharmacists, though.

Pluto in the sign of Pisces or in the twelfth house is the symbol for hard internal battle, guilt complex, ecstasy and powerful healings through the process of praying.

Made in the USA
Lexington, KY
09 July 2019